George Lowell Austin, Monthly Co Bay State

The Bay State monthly:

A Massachusetts magazine

George Lowell Austin, Monthly Co Bay State

The Bay State monthly:
A Massachusetts magazine

ISBN/EAN: 9783337732578

Printed in Europe, USA, Canada, Australia, Japan

Cover: Foto ©ninafisch / pixelio.de

More available books at **www.hansebooks.com**

THE
BAY STATE MONTHLY.

𝔄 Massachusetts Magazine.

VOL. III.   AUGUST, 1885.   No. III.

JOHN ALBION ANDREW.

THE "WAR-GOVERNOR" OF MASSACHUSETTS.

JOHN ALBION ANDREW, the twenty-first Governor of Massachusetts, was born, May 31, 1818, at Windham, a small town near Portland, Maine. His father was Jonathan Andrew, who had established himself in Windham as a small trader; his mother was Nancy Green Pierce, of New Hampshire, who was a teacher in the celebrated academy at Frye-burg, where Daniel Webster was once employed in the same capacity.

Jonathan is described as having been "a quiet, reticent man, of much intelligence and a keen perception of the ludicrous," while his wife was "well educated, with great sweetness of temper, and altogether highly prepossessing in appearance." There never was a more united and happy family. The father possessed ample means for their education, and left his household to the good management of his wife, who was admirable in her domestic arrangements, judicious, sensible, energetic, and a rigid disciplinarian of her children. There was a rare union of gentleness and force in this woman, which made her generally attractive, and especially endeared her to all who came under the influence of her character.

Mrs. Andrew died on the 7th of March, 1832. Shortly afterwards the husband sold out his property in Windham and removed to a farm in Boxford, in the county where he was born. He died in September, 1849.

John Albion, the oldest son, entered Bowdoin College in 1833, where he pursued a course in no way remarkable. He was a studious youth, applied himself closely to his books, and appeared to take no lively interest in athletic sports. Notwithstanding his studiousness, he was ranked among the lowest of his class, and was allotted no part at Commencement.

Among his fellows he was, however, exceedingly popular, and his happy temperament, his genial nature, won him friendship which after years only made stronger and more enduring.

After his graduation the young man came to Boston and entered the office of the late Henry H. Fuller, as a student of law. The attraction between him and young Andrew was mutual, and they became almost like brothers. It was while serving his novitiate under Mr. Fuller that Andrew became interested in many of the reform movements of the day, and was as firm and peculiar in one direction as his friend was in another.

Andrew rose slowly at the bar. To his clients he simply did his duty, and that was all. He was not a learned lawyer, nor was he in any sense a great lawyer, and yet he expended great care and industry in looking up his cases, and probably never lost a client who had once employed him. We are told by one of his biographers that, "during all these years he was not what was called a student, but was never idle." He entered largely into the moral questions of that day; was greatly interested in the preaching of James Freeman Clarke; a constant attendant at meeting and the Bible-classes. Occasional lay-preaching being the custom of that church, young Andrew sometimes occupied the pulpit and conducted the services to the general acceptance of the people.

Andrew did not become actively interested in politics until his admission to the bar, and then he joined the Whig party, and became thoroughly in earnest in advocating the Anti-Slavery movement. In 1859 he was chosen to the lower branch of the Legislature and at once took a prominent position. In 1860 he was nominated for Governor of the Commonwealth, "by a general popular impulse which overwhelmed the old political managers, who regarded him as an intruder upon the arena, and had laid other plans. He was called to the position of chief magistrate of Massachusetts at a most momentous time, but he was found equal to the emergency, and early acquired, by general consent, the title of " The Great War-Governor."

It was just on the eve of the Rebellion, and the whole North was excited by the events which had already transpired. In his inaugural address in January, '61, Governor Andrew advised that a portion of the militia should be placed on a footing of activity, in order that, "in the possible contingencies of the future the State might be ready without inconvenient delay to contribute her share of force in any exigency of public danger," and immediately despatched a confidential messenger to the Governors of Maine and New Hampshire to inform them of his determination to prepare for instant service the militia of Massachusetts, and to invite their coöperation.

This is not the place nor the time to give even a *résumé* of Governor Andrew's administration. He retired from office at the close of 1865, after a service of unexampled interest and importance in the history of the Commonwealth. He retired with honor to himself and to the regret of all who had known him best. We have already alluded to Governor Andrew's interest in the question of Anti-Slavery, and it should be stated that in regard to the emancipation of the slaves he was among the first, as he was the most persistent advocate of a measure which he considered the greatest blow that could be struck at the enemy, fully justified as a measure of war and demanded by every consideration of justice and humanity.

Apropos of his impatience on this subject the following incident related by one of the Governor's friends is worth recalling : —

"It was the summer of 1862, when emancipation was being talked a great deal. We had not had any great successes, and everybody had a notion that emancipation ought to come. One day the Governor sent for me to come up to the State-House. I went up to his room, and I never shall forget how I met him. He was signing some kind of bonds, standing at a tall desk in the Council Chamber, in his shirt-sleeves, his fingers all covered with ink. He said, ' How do you do? I want you to go to Washington.' — ' Why, Governor,' said I, ' I can't go to Washington on any such notice as this ; I am busy, and it is impossible for me to go.' — ' All my folks are serving their country,' said he ; and he mentioned the various services the members of his staff were engaged in, and said with emphasis, ' Somebody must go to Washington.' — ' Well, Governor, I don't see how I can.' Said he, ' I command you to go !' — ' Well,' said I, ' Governor, put it in that way and I shall go, of course.' — ' There is something going on,' he remarked. ' This is a momentous time.' He turned suddenly towards me and said, ' You believe in prayer, don't you?' I said, ' Why, of course.' — ' Then let us pray ;' and he knelt right down at the chair that was placed there ; we both kneeled down, and I never heard such a prayer in all my life. I never was so near the throne of God, except when my mother died, as I was then. I said to the Governor, ' I am profoundly impressed ; and I will start this afternoon for Washington.' I soon found out that emancipation was in everybody's mouth, and when I got to Washington and called upon Sumner, he began to talk emancipation. He asked me to go and see the President, and tell him how the people of Boston and New England regarded it. I went to the White House that evening and met the President. We first talked about everything but emancipation, and finally he asked me what I thought about emancipation. I told him what I thought about it, and said that Governor Andrew was so far interested in it that I had no doubt he had sent me on there to post the President in regard to what the class of people I met in Boston and New York thought of it, and then I repeated to him, as I had previously to Sumner, this prayer of the Governor's, as well as I could remember it. The President said, ' When we have the Governor of Massachusetts to send us troops in the way he has, and when we have him to utter such prayers for us, I have no doubt that we shall succeed.' In September the Governor sent for me. He had a despatch that emancipation would be proclaimed, and it was done the next day. You remember the President made proclamation in September to take effect in January. Well, he and I were together alone again in the Council Chamber. Said he, ' You remember when I wanted you to go on to Washington?' I said, ' Yes, I remember it very well.' — ' Well,' said he, ' I didn't know exactly what I wanted you to go for then. Now I will tell you what let's do ; you sing " Coronation," and I'll join with you.' So we sang together the old tune, and also " Praise God from whom all blessings flow." Then I sang " Old John Brown," he marching around the room and joining in the chorus after each verse."

After the war had begun, Governor Andrew insisted on every measure to defeat the Confederate armies that was consistent with the laws of war. He was especially strenuous in demanding the emancipation of the slaves, as the following quotation from a sketch by Mr. Albert G. Browne, Jr., the Governor's military secretary, will show : —

" Over the bodies of our soldiers who were killed at Baltimore he had recorded a prayer that he might live to see the end of the war, and a vow that, so long as he should govern Massachusetts, and so far as Massachusetts could control the issue, it should not end without freeing every slave in America. He believed, at the first, in the policy of emancipation as a war measure. Finding that timid counsels controlled the government at Washington, and the then commander of the Army of the Potomac, so that there was no light in that quarter, he hailed the action of Fremont in Missouri in proclaiming freedom to the Western slaves. Through all the reverses which afterwards befell that officer he never varied from this friendship ; and when at last Fremont retired from the Army of Virginia, the Governor offered him the command of a Massachusetts regiment, and vainly urged him to take the field again under our State flag. Just so, afterwards, he welcomed the similar action of Hunter in South Carolina, and wrote in his defence the famous letter in which he urged 'to fire at the enemy's magazine.' He was deeply disappointed when the administration disavowed Hunter's act, for he had hoped much from the personal friendship which was known to exist between the General and the President. Soon followed the great reverses of McClellan before Richmond.

" The feelings of the Governor at this time, on the subject of emancipation, are well expressed in a speech which he made on Aug. 10, 1862, at the Methodist camp-meeting on Martha's Vineyard. It was the same speech in which occurs his remark since so often quoted : —

" ' I know not what record of sin awaits me in the other world, but this I know, that I was never mean enough to despise any man because he was black.'

" Referring to slavery, he said : —

" ' I have never believed it to be possible that this controversy should end and peace resume her sway until that dreadful iniquity has been trodden beneath our feet. I believe it cannot, and I have noticed, my friends (although I am not superstitious, I believe), that, from the day our government turned its back on the proclamation of General Hunter, the blessing of God has been withdrawn from our arms. We were marching on conquering and to conquer; post after post had fallen before our victorious arms; but since that day I have seen no such victories. But I have seen no discouragement. I bate not one jot of hope. I believe that God rules above, and that he will rule in the hearts of men, and that, either with our aid or against it, he has determined to let the people go. But the confidence I have in my own mind that the appointed hour has nearly come makes me feel all the more confidence in the certain and final triumph of our Union arms, because I do not believe that this great investment of Providence is to be wasted.'"

Governor Andrew retired from office January 5, 1866, and, returning to private life, he again entered upon a large practice at the bar, which was lucrative as well.

On the 30th of October, 1867, he died suddenly of apoplexy, after tea, at his own home on Charles street, Boston. The body was laid in Mount Auburn Cemetery, but was afterwards removed to the old burial-place in Hingham, where a fine statue has since been erected over his grave.

Governor Andrew was married Christmas evening, December, 1848, to Miss Eliza Jane, daughter of Charles Hersey, of Hingham. They had four children living at the time of his death, — John Forrester, born Nov. 26, 1850; Elizabeth Loring, born July 29, 1852; Edith, born April 5, 1854; Henry Hersey, born April 28, 1858.

Mr. Edwin P. Whipple, who was first chosen as the most competent person to write the biography of Governor Andrew, after examining the Governor's private and official correspondence, affirmed that he could discover nothing in his most private notes which was not honorable.

Says Mr. Peleg W. Chandler, in his "Memoir and Reminiscences of Governor Andrew,"[1] a most charming volume, from which largely this sketch has been prepared:—

"He passed more than twenty years in an arduous profession, and never earned more than enough for the decent and comfortable support of his family. He devoted his best years to the country, and lost his

BURIAL-PLACE AND MONUMENT, HINGHAM, MASS.

life in her service. His highest ambition was to do his duty in simple faith and honest endeavor, of such a character the well-known lines of Sir Henry Watton are eminently applicable:—

> " This man was free from servile bands
>   Of hope to rise, or fear to fall;
>   Lord of himself, though not of lands,
>   And having nothing, yet had all."

[1] Published by Roberts Brothers, Boston.

THE CITY OF WORCESTER — THE HEART OF THE COMMONWEALTH.

By Fanny Bullock Workman.

THE city of Worcester, forty-four miles west of Boston, lies in a valley surrounded on all sides by hills, and covers an area which may be roughly estimated as extending four miles in length by two in breadth, its long axis running north and south. It is the second city in the State in point of population, while in enterprise it yields the palm

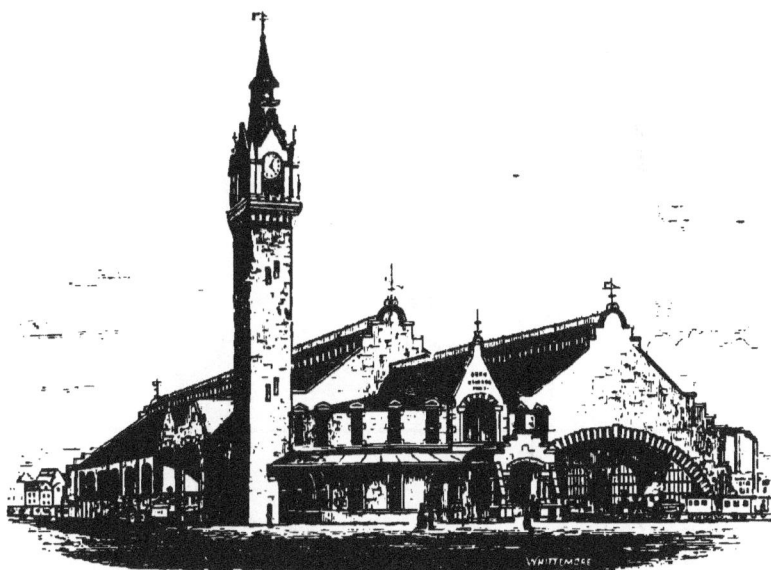

UNION PASSENGER STATION.

to none of its size in the country, sending to all parts of the world its manufactured products, the excellence of which has established the reputation of the place in which they were produced.

Worcester was first settled in the spring of 1675, under the name of Quinsigamond. The original order of the General Court, granted Oct. 11th, 1665, was as follows : —

This Court, understanding by the petition of Thomas Noyes, John Haynes of Sudbury, and Nathaniel Treadaway of Watertown, hereunto affixed, that there is a meete place for a Plantation about ten miles from Marlborow, westward, at or neer Quansetamug Pond, which, that it may be improved for that end, and not spoiled by the grantinge of farms, in answer to the forsaid petition, This Court doth order, that

FIRST UNIVERSALIST CHURCH.

there should be a quantitie of eight miles square
layd out and reserved thereabout, in the Courts
dispose, for a plantation, for the encouragement
of such persons as shall appear, any time within
three years from the date hereof, beeing men approved by this Court; and that Capt. Edward
Johnson, Lieut. Joshua ffisher, and Lieut. Thomas
Noyes, shall, and are herby appointed and
empowered to lay out the same, and to be
payd by such persons as shall appear within
the terme above expressed. The Deputies
have passed this with reference to the consent of our honored Magistrates hereto.

WILLIAM TORREY *clerk*

The Magistrates consent to a survey
of the place petitioned for, and that Capt.
Gookin doe joine with those mentioned of
our brethren the deputies, and make re-

turn of their survey to the next General
Court of Elections, who may take order
therein as they shall meete, their
brethren the deputies hereto consenting.

EDWARD RAWSON *Sec'y.*

WILLIAM TORREY *Cleric.* Consented
to by the deputies.

At that time several
persons occupied lands
that had been granted
them, and built houses.
This infant settlement
was strangled almost at
its birth by the outbreak
of King Philip's War,
which spread in that
year throughout Massa-
chusetts. The colonists,
few in number, and with-
out adequate means of
protection against the
hostile savages, soon
abandoned their build-
ings, which were burned
by the Indians, Decem-

FIRST UNITARIAN CHURCH.

ber 2, 1675. In 1684 some of the former proprietors
returned to their lands, accompanied by new settlers,
and a second plantation was formed; this time under
the name of Worcester. The records relating to the
fortunes of this plantation are very meagre; but it
continued to exist till 1700, or 1702, when, during the
progress of the French and Indian hostilities, owing
to its exposed position, it was again deserted by its
inhabitants. One man only, Digory Serjent, remained
with his family, refusing to give up to the Indians the

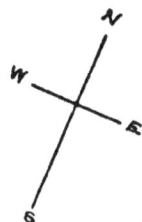

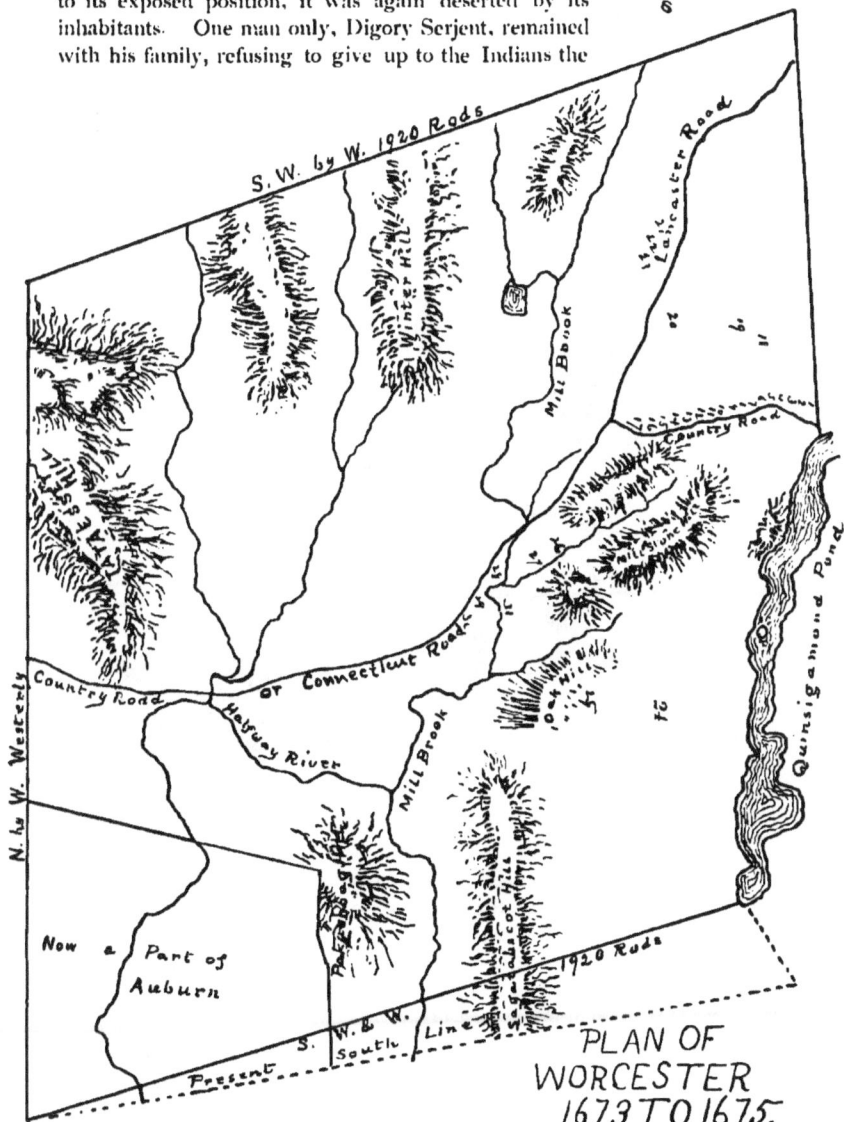

PLAN OF
WORCESTER
1673 TO 1675.

fields his labor had brought under cultivation. For a time he was unmolested. The authorities sent messengers to warn him of the danger he incurred by his rash course, and to advise his removal with his family to a place of safety. But the warning and admonition were alike disregarded. At last, early in the winter of 1702, an armed force was sent to compel him to depart. They marched with due expedition, but, being detained overnight by a severe snow-storm at a blockhouse about two miles from his residence, they arrived too late to attain their object, and found his body, scarcely yet cold, lying on the floor, and his family carried captive by the Indians. Thus terminated the second attempt at a settlement on this spot, which was again given over for several years to desolation and decay.

The principal seat of the Indians in this vicinity was Pakachoag Hill, a little south of where now stands the College of the Holy Cross. They were called

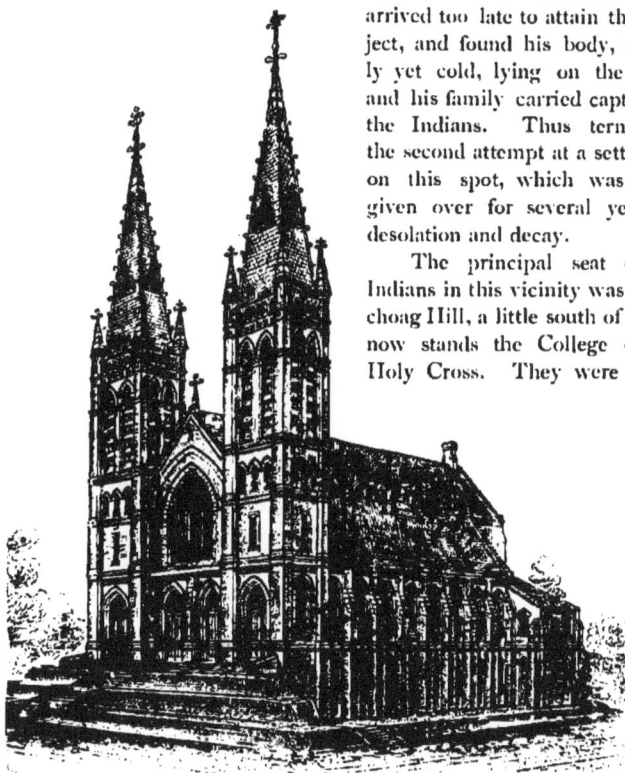

ST. PAUL'S CHURCH.

Nipmuck Indians, and consisted of about twenty families, numbering about one hundred persons, under Sagamore John. Another tribe, of about the same number, dwelt on Tatnuck Hill, under Sagamore Solomon. John Eliot, the famous apostle to the Indians, with General Daniel Gookins, visited these tribes in 1674; but he did not fully reclaim them to peaceful habits, although many of them professed Christianity.

In 1713 the inhabitants, not discouraged by their former experience, one after another returned again to take possession of their property; and this time they returned to stay. They were joined by others, and the population began to increase. In 1722 Worcester was incorporated as a town, and henceforth assumed its share of responsibility with the other towns in adopting measures for the general welfare, and contributed its proportion of men and supplies for the common defence. Through the stormy period preceding the War of the Revolution, the public sentiment of Worcester sustained the rights of the Colonies, and when, on the 19th of April, 1775, the messenger of war, on his white horse, dashed through the town, shouting, "To arms! to arms! the war is begun." the response was immediate; the bell was rung, cannon fired, and the minute-men, true to name, rallied on the Common, where they were

CHAIR MANUFACTORY OF E. W. VAILL.

THE NEW CENTRAL CHURCH

paraded by Capt. Timothy Bigelow. At about five o'clock in the afternoon they took up their line of march. Capt. Benjamin Flagg soon followed, with thirty-one men, — a total of one hundred and eight men. Capt. Bigelow having halted at Sudbury, to rest his men, was met by Capt. Flagg, when they both pushed on to Cambridge, where the organization of the army was being made. Timothy Bigelow, whose abilities were at once recognized, was appointed Major in Col. Jonathan Ward's regiment. On the 24th of

April another company, of fifty-nine men, all from Worcester, enlisted under Capt. Jonas Hubbard. During the seven dark years that followed, this town never wavered in its devotion to the cause of liberty, and was represented on many of the most important battle-fields, as well as at the surrender of Yorktown, which terminated the struggle for independence. Saturday, the 14th of July, 1776, the Declaration of Independence was received. It was publicly read, for the first time on Massachusetts soil, from the porch of the Old South Church, by Isaiah Thomas, to the assembled crowd. On Sunday, after divine service, it was read in the church. Measures were adopted for a proper celebration of the event, and on the Monday following, the earliest commemoration of the occasion, since hallowed as the national anniversary, took place in the town.

Worcester continued to increase both in size and importance during the first half of

POST-OFFICE AND MASONIC HALL.

the present century, till, in 1848, having outgrown the limits of a town, it was made a city, and the first city government inaugurated, with Ex-Gov. Levi Lincoln, Mayor, and the following Aldermen: Parley Goddard, Benjamin F. Thomas, John W. Lincoln, James S. Woodworth, William B. Fox, James Estabrook, Isaac Davis, and Stephen Salisbury. The City Clerk was Charles A. Hamilton; the City Treasurer, John Boyden; and the City Marshal, George Jones. Since then it has made rapid strides in growth, influence, and prosperity. When the call for troops to defend Washington came, in 1861, Worcester as a city was true to her record as a town; for within twelve hours a company started for the seat of war, and passed through Baltimore with the Sixth Massachusetts Regiment, on the memorable 19th of April, just eighty-six years from the first shedding of Massachusetts blood at Lexington.

In 1800 the population of Worcester was 2,411; in 1820 it was 2,962; in 1840, 7,500; in 1850, 17,049; in 1860, about 25,000; in 1870, about 41,000. At the present time it is about 70,000. The first event of consequence that gave an impetus to the growth of the town was the opening of the Blackstone Canal, in 1828, connecting Worcester with tide-water at Providence. This, although considered at the time a marvel of engineering skill, and undoubtedly of great benefit to the

WORCESTER CORSET COMPANY'S WORKS.

public, was not a successful enterprise, and on the establishment of railroads a few years later was discontinued.

In 1831 the Boston and Worcester Railroad was incorporated and soon built, followed at short intervals by the Western Railroad, the Norwich and Worcester, the Nashua and Worcester, Fitchburg and Worcester, and the Providence and Worcester railroads; thus making a centre from which one could travel in any direction. Later the Barre and Gardner Railroad was built, and the Boston and Worcester consolidated with the Western Railroad. By this last corporation the Union Passenger Station was erected, in 1877, which is one of the most costly, elegant, and convenient edifices devoted to this business in the country. About seventy-five trains arrive and depart daily. The advantage thus given to Worcester over other towns in the county was great, and the results were striking and immediate, as may be seen by reference to the figures of population above given. The facility of

communication thus afforded caused capitalists to settle here, and manufactures rapidly sprang up and flourished, drawing to this spot thousands of
laborers, who otherwise would have gone elsewhere. At the present time
the chief interests of the city centre in its manufactures, which embrace

FREE PUBLIC LIBRARY.

almost every variety of articles made in iron, steel, and wire cotton and
woollen fabrics, leather, wood, and chemicals.

Among the multitude of manufactured products it is almost useless to
attempt to specify any particular ones. The same is true of the manufacturing establishments and corporations. Mention may be made,
however, of the Washburn & Moen Wire Works, which give employment
to about three thousand operatives, established in 1831, and having a
capital of two million dollars. The power used in manufacturing is
almost exclusively steam, but water is used somewhat in the outskirts,
where streams have been dammed to make reservoirs.

Connected with the growth of Worcester it is interesting to note
that the increase in the population has been largely from the ranks of
the laboring classes. The manner in which the city is built shows this
to the most casual observer. There are but few large estates or imposing
residences, surrounded with extensive grounds. The great majority of the
houses are made of wood, are of small size, and stand in small enclos-
ures. As mechanics have prospered they have bought land, and
built such houses as were suitable to their means, obtaining loans of the
savings-banks, which they have paid off gradually. This has been
especially the case the last few years, during which time the city has ex-

tended in every direction in the manner indicated; and it is said the greater part of the deposits in the savings-banks, as well as their loans, have been made by and to people of the laboring class. This shows a general prosperity, and indicates a permanency of population not seen in many cities. During the last twenty years many people who began life with the most modest means, or with none at all, have become wealthy; and in almost every such case their prosperity has been due to their connection with manufacturing interests.

Worcester is exceptionally fortunate in its water-supply. This is derived from two large reservoirs fed by running streams, each about five miles distant from the city. One of these, called the Lynde-Brook

THE PRESENT ANTIQUARIAN HALL.

Reservoir, is situated in the township of Leicester. It was built in 1864, has a water-shed of 1,870 acres, and a storage capacity of 681,000,000 gallons, and an elevation of 481 feet above the City Hall. The dam of this reservoir gave way in February, 1876, during a freshet, and the immense mass of water was precipitated, with an unearthly roar, into the valley below, destroying everything in its path, and carrying rocks, earth, trees, and *débris* to a distance of several miles. The other, called the Holden Reservoir, is in the township of Holden. This was built in 1883, has a water-shed of 3,148 acres, a storage capacity of 450,000,000 gallons, and lies 260 feet above the City Hall. There are also three distributing reservoirs at elevations of 177 to 184 feet above the level of Main street, and supplied from the two principal reservoirs. Thirty-inch mains connect the reservoirs with the city. The height of the

water-supply gives a pressure in the pipes at the City Hall of from sixty to
seventy-five pounds to the square inch, which is sufficient to throw a stream
of water to the tops of the highest buildings,—a great advantage in case
of fire, rendering the employment of steam fire-engines unnecessary in
those parts of the city provided with hydrants. The water is of excellent
quality, being remarkably free from impurities, either organic or mineral.
The total amount expended on the water-works from 1864 to December
1, 1884, is $1,653,456, and the income from water-rates for the
year ending December, 1884, was $107,515. The uneven character of the ground upon which Worcester is built is favorable to drainage, and advantage has been taken of this fact to construct an excellent system of sewers, which thoroughly drain the greater parts of the city. All abutters are obliged to enter the sewers; and no surface-drainage nor cesspools are allowed. The result is that Worcester is a very clean city, and few places can be found either in the city itself or in the suburbs where surface accumulations exhale unpleasant or noxious odors. To the influence of pure water and good drainage may partly be ascribed the general good health of the inhab-

THE OLD SOUTH MEETING-HOUSE.

itants, and the absence, during the last few years, of anything like an
epidemic of diseases dependent upon unsanitary conditions. The sewers
all converge upon one large common sewer, which discharges its contents into the Blackstone river at Quinsigamond.

In Worcester, as in most of the smaller cities of New England, the
Main street is the chief thoroughfare and the site of many of the prominent
buildings. This street runs north and south, and is about two and a
half miles long. Near the north end, at Lincoln square, are the Court-
House and the American Antiquarian Society building. The latter
contains a large number of valuable and rare books, much sought after

for reference by students. Farther on toward the business centre are the Bay State House — Worcester's principal hotel — and Mechanics' Hall. This hall is one of the handsomest and largest in the State, and has a seating capacity of about two thousand. In the centre of the city, bordering upon Main street, is the Old Common, the original park of Worcester, now a small breathing-place of the working class, where band concerts are frequently given in summer. Here stand the Soldiers' Monument, designed by Randolph Rogers, of Rome, and the Bigelow Monument, erected to Timothy Bigelow, who commanded the minute-men who marched to Cambridge upon receipt of the news of the Battle of Lexington, and served throughout the Revolution as colonel of the Fifteenth Massachusetts Regiment. At one corner of the Common, facing Main street, is the City Hall, a small, unimposing structure, hardly worthy of the city. The question of erecting a new one has been lately agitated. Near by stands the Old South Church, built in 1763. The business

ELM PARK.

portion of Main street is well lined with large blocks, and the south end is laid out for residences.

Upon one of the hills, at the west side, stands the City Hospital, which is well managed and kept up, and has a visiting staff of the best physicians in the city. In connection with this institution, a training-school for nurses has lately been established.

The city's most imposing building is the Worcester State Lunatic Asylum, which can be seen from the trains on the Boston and Albany Railroad. A picturesque edifice in itself it crowns a hill about two miles east of Worcester, and overlooks the blue waters of Lake Quinsigamond, and also a charming stretch of hill and dale beyond. Were the softening charms of nature a potent remedy for the diseased mind, speedy cures might be effected in this sequestered retreat. It contains generally over seven hundred inmates, and can accommodate more. The building, begun in 1873, was completed in 1877, is handsomely fitted up throughout, and very spacious. It cost one million and a quarter dollars.

THE BIGELOW MONUMENT.

On Summer street is the Asylum for the Chronic Insane. For many years it was the only asylum, but upon the completion of the new building the chronic cases were removed there, and it has since been devoted to their needs only. The Technical School, or Free Institute, is situated on a pretty wooded acclivity on the west side. Founded in 1865, it was endowed, through the liberality of John Boynton, of Templeton, with $100,000, which he left as a legacy for that purpose. This school is more particularly for mechanics, chemists, and engineers, and is conducted on the plan of the polytechnic schools of Europe. It is the aim of the institution to train young men in such branches as are not usually taught in the high schools, that any mechanic or civil engineer on leaving the establishment may be fitted in a thoroughly scientific manner to pursue his life-work. The institution is free to Worcester-county residents; to those outside of the county the price of tuition is $150. The number of students accommodated is one hundred and twenty-six. The Free Public Library, founded in 1859, is one of the best in the State, has a circulating department of 26,000 and an intermediate department of 14,000 books; also a reference collection of over 20,000 volumes, bequeathed by the late Dr. John Green. An endowment fund, left by this gentleman for the latter collection, is used to the best advantage in procuring a great variety of encyclopædias and other desirable

THE WASHBURN & MOEN MANUFACTURING COMPANY.

books of reference. That Worcester citizens appreciate their opportunities in this line is indicated by the large daily patronage. Connected with the Public Library is a well-arranged reading-room, supplied with periodicals and daily papers, accessible at all times to the public; also the valuable library of the Worcester District Medical Society, containing about 6,000 volumes. The able and accomplished librarian is Mr. S. S. Green, who not only supplies its shelves with the newest and most desirable books for reading and reference, but is a fountain-head of information in himself, and ever ready and willing to answer the many questions put to him constantly by a steady concourse of applicants.

The public-school system has been the occasion of much compliment, and is regarded both here and elsewhere as a model one. In 1733 it was voted, "that a school-house be built in the centre half, and that said school house be 24 feet long, 16 feet wide, and 7 feet stud, and be completely finished with good chimney glass." This was the first school-house built in Worcester, and it stood at the north end of Main street, near the middle of the present street, and there remained until after the close of the Revolution. In 1740 £100 were granted for the support of schools. The first Grammar school was established in 1752. In 1755 John Adams, afterward President of the United States, taught the Latin Grammar school here, and remained until 1758. There are now twenty-six different school-houses, including the High School, a large effective building, situated on Walnut street. Further accommodations at the present time are greatly needed, the existing houses being overcrowded. The amount last appropriated for the schools was $184,500 for maintenance, and $20,000 for the purchase of free text-books. Beside the public schools there are several large and well-known educational institutions, — the College of the Holy Cross, the Free Institute, the Worcester Academy, the Highland Military Academy, the Oread Insti-

OLD PAINE HOMESTEAD, LINCOLN STREET

tute, the State Normal School, and the Roman Catholic Parochial schools. There are also several private schools of note. The educational interests of the city have kept pace with its rapid and astonishing growth.

Worcester has seven national banks, four savings-banks, and one safety deposit and trust company.

Among a number of newspapers the chief ones have been the " Spy " and " Evening Gazette." The " Massachusetts Spy " is one of the oldest papers in this country, and has been published with unbroken numbers for 115 years. It was established in Boston, in July, 1770, but was removed to Worcester by its proprietor, Isaiah Thomas, in May, 1775. It was in those days outspoken with regard to the difficulties between the mother country and the colonies, and, owing to its urgent appeals for freedom from tyranny, it became necessary to remove press and paper. Mr. Thomas was certainly one of the most remarkable men of his day. His patriotism never waned

during the most trying days of the Revolution, and the " Massachusetts Spy "
and its editor are a part of the history of the country. July 22, 1845, the
" Daily Spy " was first issued. The first number was on a sheet 18 by 23
inches, a trifle larger than the first number of the " Massachusetts Spy," which
was 16 by 20 inches. It has been enlarged several times. The " National
Ægis," published in 1801, in 1833 merged into the " Massachusetts Yeoman,"

HIGH SCHOOL BUILDING.

a paper started in 1823. The name was changed to the " Worcester Palladium." In 1829 the " Worcester County Republican " was started, and also
merged into the " Palladium," in 1834. It was a successful paper for years,
but in 1876 it was sold to the " Spy." The " Gazette," begun in 1801 as a
weekly, became a daily in 1843, and is now an eight-page paper, the only
one in the city. In 1851 the " Daily Morning Transcript " was issued.
Early in 1866 its name was changed to the " Evening Gazette," and it is
now the representative afternoon sheet of the city. There are two able and
well-conducted French weekly journals, — " Le Travailleur," and " Le
Courier de Worcester."

In 1719 the first church was built, near the present Old South Church,
on Main street. Previous to that time the inhabitants had held service in their
different houses, where their prayers were often interrupted by the presence

of hostile Indians, who took the occasion when the people were absorbed in their devotions to molest them. In 1763 the present Old South Meeting-House was built. The original dimensions were seventy feet long, fifty-five wide, with a tower on the north side surmounted by a spire one hundred and thirty feet high. It was commenced June 21, 1763, and first occupied Dec. 8, 1763. There were sixty-one large square box pews and seven long ones on each side of the broad aisle, which were free. The building committee consisted of John Chandler, Joshua Bigelow, Josiah Brewer, John Curtis, James Putnam, Daniel Boyden, James Goodwin, Jacob Hemmenway, David Bigelow, Samuel Moore, and Elisha Smith. The entire expense of the building was £1,542.

Since the date of its erection there have been many changes and additions, so that it now presents but little of the appearance of its former self.

The bell now in use was cast in 1802, and has this inscription : —

> " The living to the church I call,
> And to the grave I summon all."

In 1786, owing to certain disagreements, a division occurred in the parish, some of its members leaving and forming an organization of their own, with the Rev. Mr. Bancroft as rector. This society dedicated its first church January 1, 1722, and this was replaced by a new structure, of brick, in 1829, which is still in use. Since this first division new societies have sprung up and new churches have been built, until to-day there are forty-eight different houses of worship, among which are eleven Congregational, eight Methodist Episcopal, seven Baptist, seven Roman Catholic, three Protestant Episcopal, two Universalist, and two Unitarian churches.

On account of the encircling hills the climate of Worcester is hot in summer, but somewhat more temperate and less subject to east winds in winter than that of Boston.

The surrounding country has all the charms that cultivated soil and undulating hill-and-valley scenery can give. Good roads run in various directions to the adjacent towns, and strangers often speak of the many different and delightful drives to be found about Worcester.

Three miles east of the city is the beautiful sheet of water called Lake Quinsigamond. It is a narrow lake, about five miles long, with thickly wooded banks, and its surface dotted with picturesque little islands. Along its shores the Nipmuck Indians are said to have lived and hunted ; and on Wigwam Hill, a wooded eminence overlooking the water, where one of their encampments is supposed to have been, are still occasionally found specimens of their rude house utensils.

A large tract of land bordering on the lake has lately been given to the city by two Worcester gentlemen, and it is expected that in the near future it will be cleared away and made into a public park. The only park that the city now possesses, besides the Common, before alluded to, is a small affair on the west side, at the foot of Elm street, one of the principal residence streets.

ABRAHAM LINCOLN.

BY GEORGE LOWELL AUSTIN.

THERE is something eminently satisfactory in the reflection that, when the new faith, "That all men are created equal," and that "Governments are instituted among men deriving their just powers from the consent of the governed," was finally assailed by the slave-power of America, and had to pass the ordeal of four years of war, a man born and reared in poverty, deficient in education, unused to the etiquette even of ordinary society, and untutored in the art of diplomacy and deception, had been selected by the people of the United States to become the representative of the new faith, and the defender of the government established upon it. This man was ABRAHAM LINCOLN, of Illinois, the record of whose life, at once important, eventful, and tragic, it is pleasant to recall.

There are, in my judgment, at least four men associated with the period of the civil war, who, in their early lives, their struggles, their training, and their future callings, ought forever to command the admiration of this people : Lincoln, the lowly, the exalted, the pure man in rude marble, the plain cover to a gentle nature, the giant frame and noble intellect; Grant, the defender of the Federal Union, the unflinching soldier, around whose dying couch a whole nation now lingers, whose light will shine down through future ages a warning to conspirators, to freemen a pledge, and to the oppressed a beacon of hope; Stanton, the lion of Buchanan's cabinet, the collaborator of Lincoln, the supporter of Grant, gifted with the far-seeing eye of a Carnot, spotless in character, incorruptible in integrity, great in talent and learning, and a fit object of unhesitating trust; and John Rogers, the American sculptor, who has offered, in his beautiful and famous group of statuary, "The Council of War," an undying tribute to these three great leaders in American history, and is himself worthy to be grouped with them in our remembrance.

> " Leaves have their time to fall,
> And flowers to wither at the north wind's breath,
> And stars to set; but all —
> Thou hast all seasons for thine own, O Death ! "

If we could have looked into a rude log-cabin in Hardin county, Kentucky, on the morning of the 12th of February, 1809, we should have seen an infant just born, — and with what promise of future greatness? Looking ahead ten years, we should have discerned this infant, Abraham, developing into youth, still living in the old log-cabin, with neither doors nor windows, with wolves and bears for neighbors, with a shiftless father,

But his mother was dead! Still this mother had left her impress, and she had become in that boy's heart "an angel of a mother." She made him what he afterwards proved himself to be. Follow Abraham Lincoln where we will,—from the cradle to the grave,—and we shall find honesty and kindness ever distinguishing him. In his boyhood, among boys, he was always fighting the battle of the offended and the weak; in manhood, he was always protecting the fugitive from an angry mob; as a lawyer, saving the widow's son from the gallows, and declining the rich fee of an unrighteous cause; as a public debater, the fairest ever met in the political arena; and as president of the republic, honest in his convictions and kind to his bitterest enemies.

Let us not forget the difficulties which it was his lot and his good fortune to surmount. He never was six months at school in his life; and yet, by the use of a single book and the occasional aid of a village schoolmaster, he became an expert surveyor in six weeks! At the age of twenty-one he accompanied his family to Illinois. One morning, when seated at the breakfast-table of his employer, Lincoln was told that a man living six miles away had a copy of an English grammar. He left the table at once, and went and borrowed the book. During the long winter evenings that followed, in the light of the village cooper's shop, he pored over the pages of that book, — studying the science of language, the theory of human speech, and qualifying himself to become the author of one of the three great State papers of modern times, by the light of burning shavings!

But we leave that early life of his, which, in rude simplicity, repeats "the short and simple annals of the poor."

In 1832 Black Hawk, the celebrated Indian chief, then in his sixty-seventh year, crossed the Mississippi to regain the Rock River valley, — the scene of his early trials and triumphs. His coming meant war upon the pale-faced stranger, that had ventured to possess the hunting-grounds of the red men. Several companies of volunteers were raised to meet him, and Abraham Lincoln served as captain of one of them.

When the war was over Lincoln returned to New Salem, his home in Illinois, and shortly afterwards began the study of the law. He was still poor in purse, his clothing was threadbare, but his ambition was immense. He often pursued his study in the shade of a tree. One day Squire Godbey — a very good man he was, too, so we are told — saw him seated on a pile of wood, absorbed in a book, when, according to the squire, the following dialogue took place: "Says I, 'Abe, what are you studying?'—'Law,' says he. 'Great God Almighty!' says I." Studying law astride of a wood-pile, probably barefooted, was too great a shock for the squire's susceptible nature. He continued to study, then to practise a little without fee, and finally was admitted to the bar in 1836.

Judge Davis, once on the Supreme Bench of the United States, a man spotless alike upon the throne of justice and in his daily walk, was upon intimate terms with Lincoln for upwards of twenty years, and during more than half of that period sat upon the judicial bench before which Lincoln most frequently practised. No one is abler than he to speak of Lincoln as a lawyer, — a lawyer who became one of the first of the Western bar, — a bar that can proudly point to its Carpenter, its Trumbull, its Ryan, and its Davis. He says : —

"The framework of Lincoln's mental and moral being was honesty ; and a wrong cause was poorly defended by him. The ability which some eminent lawyers possess of explaining away the bad points of a cause by ingenious sophistry was denied him. In order to bring into full activity his great powers it was necessary that he should be convinced of the right and justice of the matter which he advocated. When so convinced, whether the cause was great or small, he was usually successful.

"He hated wrong and oppression everywhere ; and many a man whose fraudulent conduct was undergoing review in a court of justice has writhed under his terrific indignation and rebukes. He was the most simple and unostentatious of men in his habits, having few wants, and those easily supplied."

In 1837 Mr. Lincoln removed to Springfield, Ill., where he entered into partnership with his old friend, John T. Stuart; and this partnership continued until 1841. In 1834 he had been elected to the Legislature, and after his removal to Springfield he was again chosen to that body. It was during this period that he found the nerve, when it did require courage, to express and record his protest against the injustice of slavery. Twice as a youth he had made a trip to New Orleans, — in 1828 and 1831, — and on his second visit had for the first time observed slavery in its most brutal and revolting form. He had gone into the very centre of a slave mart, had seen families sold, the separation forever of husband and wife, of parent and child. When we recall how deeply he always sympathized with suffering, brute as well as human, and his strong love of justice, we can realize how deeply he was affected by these things. His companions on this trip have attempted to describe his indignation and grief. They said, "His heart bled. He was mad, thoughtful, abstracted, sad, and depressed."

The years which Mr. Lincoln passed in Springfield were the preparatory years of his future greatness. From this time onward he was ever a busy man.

He was once associated with Mr. Swett in defending a man accused of murder. He listened to the testimony which witness after witness gave against his client until his honest heart could stand it no longer; then, turning to his associate, he said: "Swett, the man is guilty; you defend him: I can't." Swett *did* defend him, and the man was acquitted. When proffered his share of the large fee Lincoln most emphatically declined it, on the ground that "all of it belonged to Mr. Swett, whose ardor and eloquence saved a *guilty* man from justice."

At another time, when a would-be client had stated the facts of his case,

Mr. Lincoln replied: "Yes; there is no reasonable doubt but I can gain your case for you. I can set a whole neighborhood at loggerheads. I can distress a widowed mother and her six fatherless children, and thereby get for you $600, which rightfully belongs, it seems to me, as much to the woman and her children as it does to you. You must remember that some things that are *legally* right are not *morally* right. I shall not take your case, but will give you a little advice, for which I will charge you nothing. You appear to be a sprightly, energetic man: I would advise you to try your hand at making $600 some other way."

I turn now to another phase of his nature, and recall that he had not grown up to manhood without the usual experiences of the tender passion. It was while he was yet living at New Salem that his heart opened to a fair, sweet-tempered, and intelligent girl, with the romantic name of Anne Rutledge. They were engaged to be married as soon as he should be admitted to the bar of the Supreme Court. But in August, 1835, she died. Her beauty and her attractions and her early death made a very deep impression upon him. We are told that he idealized her memory, and in his recollections of her there was a poetry of sentiment, which might possibly have been lessened, had she lived, by the prosaic realities of life. With all his love of fun and frolic, with all his wit and humor, with all his laughter and anecdotes, Lincoln, from his youth, was a man of deep feeling. We have it on the authority of the most reliable of his biographers, that he always associated with the memory of Anne Rutledge the poem which, in his hours of despondency, he so often repeated : —

"Oh! why should the spirit of mortal be proud?
Like a swift fleeting meteor, a fast flying cloud,
A flash of the lightning, a break of the wave,
He passeth from life to his rest in the grave.

"The leaves of the oak and the willow shall fade,
Be scattered around, and together be laid;
And the young and the old, and the low and the high,
Shall moulder to dust and together shall lie."

I never read this beautiful poem, so full of the true philosophy of life, so suggestive of the rich promises of the hereafter, that I do not think of the great president. He first found it in the columns of a newspaper, cut it out, carried it in his pocket, and treasured it in his memory for many years without knowing who was its author.

It would be pleasant to trace the years spent by Mr. Lincoln in the State Legislature, and to revert to some of the speeches and occasional addresses belonging to those years, which, in the light of his subsequent history, are strangely significant. In the early period of his legislative career he became acquainted with Stephen A. Douglas, while the latter was a school-teacher at Winchester. Douglas was a man of extraordinary powers, and one of the readiest of the American debaters of his time. As the years went on he became actively interested in politics, and at length assumed the leadership of the Democrats in Illinois, while Lincoln became the standard-bearer of the Whigs. When party platforms were promulgated, upon the eve of important contests, these two statesmen, by the unanimous consent of their supporters, were selected to debate the merits of their respective political creeds before the people. A series of joint discussions was arranged to take place in the various important towns of the State. The assemblages were large, and were composed of men of all parties. The discussion opened with a speech of an hour, from one of the debaters; the other replied in an address of an hour and a half; a rejoinder of half an hour brought the discussion to a close. At the next meeting the order of speaking was reversed, and by this arrangement the "last word" was indulged in alternately by each debater.

During the various joint discussions held between the eloquent political orators who were chosen to represent the Anti-Slavery and Democratic parties, it may fairly be asserted that Lincoln opposed, while Douglas defended, directly or indirectly, the slave interests of the country. The former always felt that slavery was wrong, and in seeking a remedy for the existing evil he followed in the footprints of Henry Clay. He advocated gradual emancipation, with the consent of the people of the slave States, and at the expense of the General Government. In his great speech against the Kansas and Nebraska bill, he said, "Much as I hate slavery, I would consent to its extension rather than see the Union dissolved, just as I would consent to any great evil to avoid a greater one."

The debates between Lincoln and Douglas, especially those of the year 1858, were unquestionably the most important in American history. The speeches of Mr. Lincoln, as well as of the "Little Giant" who opposed him, were circulated and read throughout the Union, and did more than any other agency to create the public opinion which prepared the way for the overthrow of slavery. As another has said, "The speeches of John Quincy Adams and of Charles Sumner were more scholarly; those of Lovejoy and Wendell Phillips were more vehement and impassioned; Senators Seward, Hale, Trumbull, and Chase spoke from a more conspicuous forum; but Lincoln's were more philosophical, while as able and earnest as any, and his manner had a simplicity and directness, a clearness of statement and felicity of illustration, and his language a plainness and Anglo-Saxon strength, better adapted than any other to reach and influence the common people, — the mass of the voters."

From 1847 to March 4, 1849, Mr. Lincoln served a term in Congress, where he acted with his party in opposing the Mexican war. In 1855 he was a prominent candidate for the United States Senate, but was defeated. From the ruins of the old Whig party and the acquisition of the Abolitionists, the Republican had been formed, and of this party, in Illinois, Mr. Lincoln became, in 1858, the senatorial candidate. Again he was defeated, by his adversary Mr. Douglas. Lincoln felt aggrieved, for he had carried the popular vote of his State by nearly

4,000 votes. When questioned by a friend upon this delicate point, he said that he felt "like the boy that stumped his toe,—it hurt him too much to laugh, and he was too big to cry."

In his speech at Springfield, with which the campaign of 1858 opened, Mr. Lincoln made the compromisers of his party tremble by enunciating a doctrine which, they claimed, provoked defeat. He said: " 'A house divided against itself cannot stand.' I believe this Government cannot permanently endure half slave and half free. I do not expect the Union to be dissolved; I do not expect the house to fall; but I do expect it will cease to be divided. It will become all one thing or all the other; either the opponents of slavery will arrest the further spread of it, and place it where the public mind shall rest in the belief that it is in a course of ultimate extinction, or its advocates will push it forward till it shall become alike lawful in all the States, —old as well as new, North as well as South."

These were prophetic words; and they were spoken by a man born in the slave State of Kentucky. It was the truth, the fearless truth, uttered in advance of even the acknowledged leader of the Republican party, Governor Seward, of New York. The simple assertion of that truth cost Lincoln a seat in the United States Senate; but it set other men's minds to thinking, and in 1860 the PEOPLE, following the path made through the forest of error by a pioneer in the cause of truth, came to similar conclusions, and made "Honest Old Abe" Chief Magistrate of the republic.

On the 10th of May, 1860, the Republican convention of Illinois met at Decatur, in Macon county, to nominate State officers and appoint delegates to the National Presidential Convention. Decatur was not far from where Lincoln's father had settled and worked a farm in 1830, and where young Abraham Lincoln and Thomas Hanks had split the rails for enclosing the old pioneer's first cornfield. Mr. Lincoln was present, simply as an observer, at the convention. Scarcely had he taken his seat when General Oglesby arose, and remarked that an old Democrat of Macon county desired to make a contribution to the convention. Two old fence rails were then brought in, bearing the inscription: " Abraham Lincoln, the rail candidate for the Presidency in 1860. Two rails from a lot of three thousand, made in 1830, by Thomas Hanks and Abe Lincoln, whose father was the first pioneer of Macon county."

The effect of this contribution can well be imagined; at once it became useless to talk in Illinois of any other man than Abraham Lincoln for President.

On the 16th of May the National Republican Convention was called together in Chicago. The convention met in a large building called the "Wigwam," which had been constructed specially for the occasion. The contest for the nomination lay between William H. Seward of New York and Abraham Lincoln of Illinois. On the third ballot, as we know, the latter was nominated. I was but a youth on that memorable day, but I vividly recollect that I was standing, with other urchins, nearly opposite the "Wigwam," and was startled when a man stationed on top of the building yelled out, "Fire: Lincoln is nominated!" Then followed the roar of cannon and cheers upon cheers.

When the news reached Mr. Lincoln he was chatting with some friends in the office of the "Sangamon Journal," in Springfield. He read the telegram aloud, and then said: "There is a little woman down at our house who will like to hear this. I'll go down and tell her." The "little woman" was his wife, whom, as Mary Todd, he had won in 1842, and he knew that she was more anxious that he should be President than he himself was.

On the 7th of November, 1860, it was known throughout the country that Lincoln had been elected. From that very hour dates the conspiracy which, by easy stages and successive usurpations of authority, culminated in rebellion. It is painful now to revert to the events which marked its progress. There is not a man living to-day, I trust, that does not wish they could be blotted out from our history. While watching the course of these events Mr. Lincoln chanced one day to be talking with his friend, Newton Bateman, a highly respectable and Christian gentleman, and Superintendent of Public Instruction in Illinois. I can only quote a part of the interview, as furnished by Mr. Bateman himself: "I know there is a God," said Lincoln; "and he hates injustice and slavery. I see the storm coming. I know that his hand is in it. If he has a place and work for me, — and I think he has, — I believe I am ready. I am nothing; but truth is everything. I know I am right, because I know that liberty is right; for Christ teaches it; and Christ is God. I have told them that 'a house divided against itself cannot stand,' and Christ and reason say the same; and they will find it so.

"Douglas doesn't care whether slavery is voted up or down; but God cares, and humanity cares, and I care; and with God's help I shall not fail. I may not see the end, but it will come, and I shall be vindicated; and these men will find that they have not read their Bible aright."

We are told that, after a pause, he resumed: "Does it not appear strange that men can ignore the moral aspects of this contest? A revelation could not make it plainer to me that slavery or the Government must be destroyed. The future would be something awful, as I look at it, but for this rock on which I stand." He alluded to the Testament which he held in his hand, and which his mother — "to whom he owed all that he was, or hoped to be" — had first taught him to read.

There is nothing in history more pathetic than the scene when, on the 11th of February, 1861, Abraham Lincoln bade a last farewell to his home of a quarter of a century.

To his friends and neighbors he said, while grasping them by the hand, "I go to assume a task more difficult than that which has devolved upon any other man since the days of Washington. He never would have succeeded except for the aid of Divine Providence, upon which he at all times relied.   I feel that I cannot succeed without the same divine blessing which sustained him, and on the same Almighty Being I place my reliance for support." The profound religious feeling which pervades this farewell speech characterized him to the close of his life.

All along the route Lincoln preached the gospel of confidence, conciliation, and peace.   Notwithstanding the ominous signs of the times, he had such an abiding faith in the people as to believe that the guarantees of all their rights under the Constitution, of non-intervention with the institution of slavery where it existed, and the assurance of a most friendly spirit on the part of the new President would calm the heated passion of the men of the South, would reclaim States already in secession, and would retain the rest of the cotton States under the banner of the Union.   What a striking evidence of the lingering hope and of the tender heart of the President is afforded by his first inaugural address !

"In your hands, my dissatisfied fellow-countrymen, and not in mine, is the momentous issue of civil war.

"The Government will not assail you.   You can have no conflict without being yourselves the aggressors; you can have no oath registered in heaven to destroy the Government, while I shall have the most solemn one, — 'to preserve, protect, and defend it.'

"I am loath to close.   We are not enemies, but friends.   We must not be enemies.   Though passion may have strained, it must not break, our bonds of affection.

"The mystic chords of memory, stretching from every battle-field and patriot grave to every living heart and hearth-stone all over this broad land, will yet swell the chorus of the Union when again touched, as surely they will be, by the better angels of our nature."

Abraham Lincoln took the helm of government in more dangerous times and under more difficult and embarrassing circumstances than any of the fifteen presidents who preceded him.   The ship of Union was built and launched and first commanded by Washington.

> "He knew what master laid her keel,
> What workmen wrought her ribs of steel,
> Who made each mast, and sail, and rope,
> What anvils rang, what hammers beat,
> In what a forge and what a heat
> Were shaped the anchors of her hope."

The men whom he chose as her first crew were those who had helped to form her model.   During succeeding generations inefficient hands were occasionally shipped to take the place of worn-out members of the original crew.   Often the vessel was put out of her course to serve the personal ends of this or that sailor, and ere long mutiny broke out among her passengers, headed by John C. Calhoun, of South Carolina.   Finally, a man ignorant in the science of astronomy and navigation, feeble alike in heart and arm, became, nominally, commander, but really the cat's-paw, of his crew, at whose bidding the ship was steered. When Abraham Lincoln was called to the helm he found the once stanch, strong vessel in a leaky, damaged condition, with her compasses deranged, her rudder broken, and the luminous star by which Washington guided his course dimmed by a cloud of disunion and doubt. When the belching cannon opened upon Sumter, then it was that the ship of State was found to be all but stranded on the shoals, — Treason.

We are all aware of the story of that struggle. We can never forget the story, for there is yet a " vacant chair," that recalls it in many a home. The manner in which President Lincoln conducted the affairs of the government during that struggle forms an important chapter in the history of the world for that period. After Good Friday comes Easter; after the day of dejection and doubt comes the day of recompense and rejoicing. To my mind there is that in the life-work of President Lincoln which itself consecrates every soldier's grave, and makes the tenant of that grave more worthy of his sublime dying. It added honor to honor to have fallen, serving under such a commander.

It was midsummer, 1862, and at a time when the whole North was depressed, that the President convened his cabinet to talk over the subject-matter of the Emancipation Proclamation. On the 22d of September ensuing it was published to the world. It was the act of the President alone. It exhibited far-seeing sagacity, courage, independence, and statesmanship. The final proclamation was issued on the 1st of January, 1863. On that day the President had been receiving calls, and for hours shaking hands. As the paper was brought to him by the Secretary of State to be signed, he said, " Mr. Seward, I have been shaking hands all day, and my right hand is almost paralyzed. If my name ever gets into history it will be for this act, and my whole soul is in it. If my hand trembles when I sign the proclamation those who examine the document hereafter will say, ' He hesitated.' " Then, resting his arm a moment, he turned to the table, took up the pen, and slowly and firmly wrote, ABRAHAM LINCOLN. He smiled as, handing the paper to Mr. Seward, he said " That will do."

This was the pivotal act of his administration; but this humane and just promise to liberate four millions of slaves, to wipe out a nation's disgrace, was followed by the darkest and most doubtful days in the history of America. Grant, in the lowlands of Louisiana, was endeavoring, against obstacles, to open the Mississippi; but, with all his energy, he accomplished nothing. McClellan's habit of growling at the President had become intolerable, and Burnside superseded him in command of the Army of the Potomac. Burnside advanced against Lee, fought him at Fredericksburg, and was repulsed with terrible disaster. Then the army broke camp for another campaign, the elements opposed, Burnside gave way to Hooker. The soldiers became disheartened, and thousands deserted to their homes in the North. The President's proclamation was now virtually a dead letter ; people looked upon it and characterized it as a joke. But there came at last a break in the clouds, and on Independence Day, 1863, the star of liberty and union appeared upon the distant sky as a covenant that God had not forsaken the Prophet of the West,— the Redeemer of the Slave. I can find no more fitting words to characterize Grant's victory at Vicksburg than those which the young and brave McPherson used in his congratulatory address to the brave men who fought for the victory : —

"The achievements of this hour will give a new meaning to this memorable day ; and Vicksburg will heighten the glory in the patriot's heart, which kindles at the mention of Bunker Hill and Yorktown. The dawn of a conquered peace is breaking before you. The plaudits of an admiring world will hail you wherever you go."

Take it altogether it was perhaps the most brilliant operation of the war, and established the reputation of Grant as one of the greatest military leaders of any age. He, the last of the triumvirate, is passing away ; and, in this connection, no apology is needed in quoting the letter which the President wrote with his own hand, and transmitted to him, on receipt of the glorious tidings : —

MY DEAR GENERAL, — I do not remember that you and I ever met personally. I write this now as a grateful acknowledgment for the almost inestimable service you have done the country. I wish to say a word further. When you first reached the vicinity of Vicksburg I thought you should do what you finally did, — march the troops across the neck, run the batteries with the transports, and then go below; and I never had any faith, except a general hope, that you knew better than I that the Yazoo-Pass expedition and the like could succeed. When you got below, and took Fort Gibson, Grand Gulf, and vicinity, I thought you should go down the river and join Gen. Banks; and when you turned northward, east of the Big Black, I thought it was a mistake. I now wish to make the personal acknowledgment that you were right, and I was wrong.

And recall now the never-to-be-forgotten scenes at Gettysburg. The Union army had been defeated at Chancellorsville, and Gen. Lee, having assumed the offensive, had been making the greatest preparations for striking a decisive blow. Already had he passed through Maryland ; he was now in Pennsylvania. But valiant men were there to meet and oppose. The fate of the day, the fate of the Confederacy, was staked upon the issue. I cannot picture the battle ; but we all know the result, and how great was the rejoicing in the North when, on that 4th day of July, the tidings of the fall of Vicksburg and the victory at Gettysburg reached the country.

A portion of the battle-field of Gettysburg was set apart as a resting-place for the heroes who fell on that bloody ground. In November of that year the ceremony of consecration took place. Edward Everett, the orator and the scholar, delivered the oration ; it was a polished specimen of his consummate skill. After him rose President Lincoln,— " simple, rude, his care-worn face now lighted and glowing with intense feeling." He simply read the touching speech which is already placed among the classics of our language : —

"Fourscore and seven years ago our fathers brought forth upon this continent a new nation, conceived in liberty, and dedicated to the proposition that all men are created equal.

"Now we are engaged in a great civil war, testing whether that nation, or any nation so conceived and so dedicated, can long endure. We are met on a great battle-field of that war. We are met to dedicate a portion of it as the final resting-place of those who here gave their lives that that nation might live. It is altogether fitting and proper that we should do this.

"But, in a larger sense, we cannot dedicate, we cannot consecrate, we cannot hallow, this ground. The brave men, living and dead, who struggled here, have consecrated it far above our power to add or detract. The world will little note, nor long remember, what we *say* here; but it can never forget what they *did* here. It is for us, the living, rather, to be dedicated here to the unfinished work that they have thus far so nobly carried on. It is rather for us to be here dedicated to the great task remaining before us, that from these honored dead we take increased devotion to the cause for which they here gave the last full measure of devotion; that we here highly resolve that the dead shall not have died in vain; that the nation shall, under God, have a new birth of freedom, and that government of the people, by the people, and for the people shall not perish from the earth."

There have been but four instances in history in which great deeds have been celebrated in words as immortal as themselves : the epitaph upon the dead Spartan band at Thermopylæ; the words of Demosthenes on those who perished at Marathon; the speech of Webster in memory of those who laid down their lives at Bunker Hill; and these words of Lincoln on the hill at Gettysburg. As he closed, and while his listeners were still sobbing, he grasped the hand of Mr. Everett, and said, "I congratulate you on your success."—"Ah," replied the orator, gracefully, "Mr. President, how gladly would I exchange all my hundred pages to have been the author of your twenty lines! "

I forbear to dwell longer on the events of the war. The tide had turned, and the end was already foreseen. Notwithstanding that Mr. Lincoln had proved the righteousness of his course, a great many people in the North — and many even in his own party — were opposed to his nomination for a second term. The disaffected nominated Gen. Fremont, upon the platform of the suppression of the Rebellion, the Monroe doctrine, and the election of President and Vice-President by the direct vote of the people, and for one term only. The Democratic party declared the war for the Union a failure, and very properly nominated McClellan. It required a long time for the General to make up his mind in regard to accepting the nomination; and, in conversations upon the subject with a friend, Lincoln suggested that perhaps he might be *entrenching.* The election was held, and Lincoln received a majority greater than was ever before given to a candidate for the presidency. The people this time were like the Dutch farmer, — they believed that " it was not best to swap horses when crossing a stream."

On the 4th of March, 1865, he delivered that memorable inaugural address which is truly accounted one of the ablest state papers to be found in the archives of America. It concludes with these words : —

" With malice towards none, with charity for all, with firmness in the right as God gives us to see the right, let us finish the work we are in, — to bind up the nation's wounds, to care for him who shall have borne the battle, and for his widow and his orphans, to do all which may achieve and cherish a just and lasting peace among ourselves and with all nations."

Read and reread this whole address.   Since the days of Christ's Sermon on the Mount, where is the speech of ruler that can compare with it ?   No other in American annals has so impressed the people. Said a distinguished statesman from New York, on the day of its de-livery, " A century from to-day that inaugural will be read as one of the most sublime utterances ever spoken by man. Washington is the great man of the era of the Revolution. So will Lincoln be of this ; but Lincoln will reach the higher position in history."

Four years before, Mr. Lincoln, an untried man, had assumed the reins of government ; now, he was the faithful and beloved servant of the people.   Then, he was ridiculed and caricatured ; and some persons even found fault with his dress, just as the British ambassador found fault with the dress of the author of the Declaration of Independence. The ambassador is forgotten, but Jefferson will live as long as a gov-ernment of the people, by the people, and for the people, endures. While he lived Lincoln was shamefully abused by the people and press of the land of his forefathers ; and not until the shot was fired-—not until the blood of the just — the ransom of the slave — was spilled, did England throw off the cloak of prejudice, and acknowledge —

> " This king of princes-peer,
> This rail-splitter, a true-born king of men."

It is well known that not all of Mr. Lincoln's friends invariably har-monized with his views.   Of the number of these Horace Greeley stood foremost, and undoubtedly caused the President great anxiety upon several occasions.   He never did things by halves ; and, whenever he undertook to do a thing, the whole country, believing in the honesty and purity of his motives, gave to him a willing ear.   From the editorial sanctum of the " Tribune" many a sharp and soul-stirring letter went forth addressed to the executive of the nation.   Mr. Lincoln read them, oftentimes replied to them, but very rarely heeded the counsel which they contained.   When the President was struck down, Mr. Greeley, who dif-fered so widely from him, mourned the loss of a very dear friend.

Charles Sumner often differed from the President, and on the floor of the

Senate Chamber frequently gave utterance to statements which carried grief into the White House. But Mr. Lincoln knew and understood Charles Sumner. An incident may here be recalled. The President was solicitous that his views, as embodied in an act then claiming the attention of Congress, should become law prior to the adjournment of that body on the 4th of March. Mr. Sumner opposed the bill, because he thought it did not sufficiently guard the interests of the freedmen of that State. Owing to the opposition of the Senator and a few of his friends the bill was defeated. Mr. Lincoln felt displeased, and the newspapers throughout the country published that the friendship which had so long existed between the two men was at an end.

But Mr. Lincoln was not a man who would withdraw friendship on account of an honest difference of opinion. It was not he who made the mistake of urging the dismissal of Mr. Sumner from the chairmanship of the Senate Committee on Foreign Relations. On the 4th of March Mr. Lincoln was reinaugurated; on the evening of the 6th occurred the Inauguration Ball. Mr. Sumner had never attended one of these state occasions, and he did not purpose doing so at this time until he received, in the course of the afternoon, the following letter: —

DEAR MR. SUMNER, — Unless you send me word to the contrary, I shall this evening call with my carriage at your house, to take you with me to the Inauguration Ball.

Sincerely yours,

ABRAHAM LINCOLN.

The great Senator entered the ball-room, with Mrs. Lincoln leaning on his arm, and took his seat by the side of the President. The evening was pleasantly spent, and the newspapers at once discovered how great a blunder they had made.

At length the curtain fell upon the bloody scenes of the war. Under the mighty blows of Grant and his lieutenants the Rebellion was crushed. On a bright day the President, accompanied by Mr. Sumner, entered the streets of Richmond, and witnessed the grateful tears of thousands of the race he had redeemed from bondage and disgrace. Having returned to Washington, he convened a cabinet council on the 14th of April. During the session his heart overflowed with kind and charitable thoughts towards the South, and towards those officers who had deserted the flag of their country in her trying hour he poured out a forgiving spirit.

After that cabinet meeting he went to drive with Mrs. Lincoln, — they two were alone. "Mary," said he, "we have had a hard time of it since we came to Washington; but the war is over, and, with God's blessing, we may hope for four years of peace and happiness, and then we will go back to Illinois and pass the rest of our lives in quiet. We have laid by some money, and during this term we will try and save up more, but shall not have enough to support us. We will go back to Illinois, and I will open a law-office at Springfield or Chicago, and practise law, and at least do enough to help give us a livelihood." Such were the dreams of

Abraham Lincoln the last day of his life. The whole world knows the remainder of the story, — of that terrible night at the theatre; of that passing away in the early dawn of the morning; of that sad and mournful passage from the Capitol to the grave at Oak Ridge Cemetery. It is painful to dwell upon it; it makes the heart faint even to recall it.

ABRAHAM LINCOLN needs no eulogy. There is but one other name in American history which can be mentioned with his as that of a peer, — the name of Washington. He was as pure, and just, and as patriotic as the Father of his Country. He was born of his time, a creature of the age of giants, a genius from the people, all the greater for his struggles, for he really did more than any man of his day to destroy caste and give courage to the lowly; and therein he wrote the brightest pages of progress. The shaft that marks his silent resting-place, the books he read, the office he used, the strong body that covered his warm heart and wise purposes, were only the outer symbols to the higher gifts of his Creator. All gifts and graces are not found in one person. He is great in whom the good predominates. All persons are not born equal. Gifts are diversified; but if ever a man had the "genius of greatness," it was Abraham Lincoln. As all are eloquent in that which they know, he was eloquent in what he both knew and did.

A few words more. The President left a heart-broken widow, a woman whose intellect was shattered by one of the most awful shocks in human history. No mind can picture the agonies which she suffered, even till the day of her death, on July 16, 1882. I make mention of her now, because, during her eventful life in Washington and afterwards, she was most cruelly treated by a portion of the press and people. I can conceive of nothing so unmanly, so devoid of every chivalric impulse, as the abuse of this poor, wounded, and bereft woman. But I am reminded of the splendid outburst of eloquence on the part of Edmund Burke, when, speaking of the heart-broken Queen of France, he said : —

"Little did I dream that I should live to see such disasters fall upon her in a nation of gallant men, — a nation of men of honor, cavaliers. I thought ten thousand swords must have leaped from their scabbards to avenge even a look that threatened her with insult. But the age of chivalry is gone."

> "Lincoln was incontestably the greatest man I ever knew. What marked him was his sincerity, his kindness, his clear insight into affairs, his firm will and clear policy. I always found him preëminently a clear-minded man. The saddest day of my life was that of Lincoln's assassination." — U. S. GRANT.

[The death of GENERAL GRANT has occurred since this article was put into type. — *Ed.*]

NANTASKET BEACH.

By Edward P. Guild.

The outline of Boston harbor somewhat resembles a very irregular letter C, with its open side facing to the north-east. The upper horn terminates with Point Shirley, in the town of Winthrop. The lower horn is a narrow ridge of land of varying width, extending four miles from the mainland, then abruptly turning to the westward for three miles. This peninsula is the town of Hull; the sharp elbow is Point Allerton.

The stretch of four miles from the point to the mainland is of greatly varying width, the harbor side being of most irregular and fantastic outline; but the side toward the sea is smooth and even, and forms Nantasket Beach, — one of the most popular watering-places on the Atlantic coast.

The development of Nantasket as a summer resort began a long time ago, although the era of large hotels and popular excursions began in the last few years. Forty or fifty years ago people from Boston, Dorchester, Hingham, and other towns, when hungering for a sniff of unalloyed sea-breeze, or a repast of the genuine clam-chowder, were in the habit of resorting to this beach, where they could pitch their tents, or find accommodations in the rather humble cottages which were already beginning to dot the shore. That the delights of the beach were appreciated then is evinced by the habitual visits of many noted men of the time, among them Daniel Webster, who often came here for recreation, usually bringing his gun with him that he might indulge his sporting proclivities; and, according to his biographer, " he was a keen sportsman. Until past the age of sixty-five he was a capital shot; and the feathered game in his neighborhood was, of course, purely wild. He used to say, after he had been in England, that shooting in ' preserves' seemed to him very much like going out and murdering the barn-door fowl. His shooting was of the woodcock, the wild-duck, and the various marsh-birds that frequent the coast of New England. . . . Nor would he unmoor his dory with his ' bob and line and sinker,' for a haul of cod or hake or haddock, without having Ovid, or Agricola, or Pharsalia, in the pocket of his old gray overcoat, for the ' still and silent hour' upon the deep."

Another frequent visitor — Peter Peregrine — wrote : " The Nantasket Beach is the most beautiful I ever saw. It sweeps around in a majestic curve, which, if it were continued so as to complete the circle, would of itself embrace a small sea. There was a gentle breeze upon the water, and the sluggish waves rolled inward with a languid movement, and broke with a low murmur of music in long lines of foam against the opposite sands. The surface of the sea was, in every direction, thickly dotted with sails; the air was of a delicious temperature, and altogether it was a scene to detain one for hours."

Evidently, Peter was a lover of nature at the sea-side; but to show that those who sojourned here forty years ago were not unexposed to ridicule, the following extract is given from a letter written from Hull in 1846: "The public and private houses at Nantasket are overrun with company, chiefly from Boston. Some of our fashionable people, as the rich are vulgarly called, will leave their airy, cool, well-appointed establishments in Boston, with every luxury the market affords, in the vain hope of finding comfort in such houses. They will leave their city palaces, the large and convenient rooms, comfortable bedsteads and mattresses, and all the delicacies of the season, and submit to being stowed away on straw-beds or cots, even upon the floor, half-a-dozen in a small chamber, or four deep in an entry, to be half-starved into the bargain upon badly cooked fish and other equally cheap commodities, for the mere sake of being able to think that they are enjoying the sea-breeze." Had the writer of this satire lived to lodge for a night in one of the palace hotels which now adorn Nantasket Beach he would have sung another song.

The peninsula of Hull is graced by three gentle elevations, — Atlantic Hill, a rocky eminence marking the southern limit of the beach; Sagamore Hill, a little farther to the north; and Strawberry Hill, about midway to Point Allerton. The last of these elevations is the most noted of the three. On its summit is an old barn, which is not only a well-known landmark for sea-voyagers, but a point of the triangulations of the official harbor surveys. In 1775 a large barn, containing eighty tons of hay, was burned on this spot by the Americans, that it might not be secured by the British. The splendid scene which this fire must have produced was doubtless applauded with even more enthusiasm than the great illuminations which are now a part of each season's events at the beach.

It is said that fierce conflicts among the savages used to often occur on the plains extending toward Point Allerton, before these parts were invaded by the white man. The theory has arisen from the finding of large numbers of skulls, bones, arrows, tomahawks, and other relics in this locality.

The trip to Nantasket from Boston by boat on a summer day is most delightful, affording a sail of an hour among the most interesting objects of Boston harbor. The point of departure is at Rowe's wharf, near the foot of Broad street, where the passenger steps on board one of the well-equipped steamers of the Boston and Hingham Steamboat Company. The course down to Nix's Mate, and thence to Pemberton, is quite straight, but the route the remainder of the way, especially after entering Weir river, is so tortuous as to cause the passenger to constantly believe that the boat is just going to drive against the shore. Upon the arrival at Nantasket pier the passenger is aware that he is at a popular resort. Barges and coaches line the long pier; ambitious porters give all possible strength of inflection to the names of their respective hotels; while innumerable *menu* cards are thrust into the visitors' hands, each calling particular attention to the chowders of the ——— House as being the best to be had on the New England coast.

Two minutes' walk is sufficient to cross from the steamboat-pier over the narrow ridge of land to the beach. The difference between one side and the other is very striking. On the one is the still, dark water of Weir river; on the other, the open sea and the rolling surf. The beach at once impresses the visitor as being remarkably fine, and, indeed, it is equalled by none on the coast, unless, possibly, by Old Orchard. The sands are hard and firm, and at low tide form a spacious boulevard for driving or walking. Before the eye is the open sea, dotted here and there with glistening sails. The long, dark vessel which appears in the distance, about four o'clock on Saturday afternoon, is a Cunard steamer, which has just left East Boston for its voyage to Liverpool. For two or three hours it is in sight, slowly and majestically moving toward the horizon.

The scene on the beach is in marked contrast to what might have been witnessed a generation ago. Then one would have found here and there a family group just driven down in the old-fashioned carryall, and enjoying a feast of clam-chowder cooked over a fire of drift-wood. Now the beach is thronged by crowds of many thousands; immense hotels vie with those of the metropolis in grandeur; there are avenues and parks, flying horses, tennis-grounds, shops for the sale of everything that the city affords, and some that it does not, dog-carts and goat-wagons, fruit and peanut-stands, bowling-alleys, shooting-targets, and, in fact, as many devices to empty the pocket-book as are usually found at a cattle-show and a church-fair together. An excursion party has just arrived, but this occurs, sometimes, several times in a day, — for Nantasket is a Mecca to the excursionist. Societies and lodges come here; clubs resort hither for a social dinner; mercantile firms send their employés on an annual sail to this place, and philanthropists provide for hundreds of poor children a day's outing on this beach.

Thus, there is no exclusiveness about Nantasket; but, at the same time, the tone of the place is excellent, and there seems to be no tendency toward its falling into disrepute, as has been the case with other very popular watering-places. It is, in fact, admitted by a New York newspaper that "Bostonians are justly proud of Nantasket Beach, where one can get cultured clams, intellectual chowder, refined lager, and very scientific pork and beans. It is far superior to our monotonous sand-beach in its picturesqueness of natural beauty, in the American character of the visitors, and in the reasonableness of hotel charges, as well as the excellence of the service."

The oldest of the large hotels now in existence at the beach is the Rockland House, which was opened in 1854 by Colonel Nehemiah Ripley, who was proprietor for many years. At first, it had forty rooms; it now has about two hundred, and is beautifully furnished. It stands at the head of a broad, rising lawn, and from its balconies and windows the view of the sea is magnificent. It is now in the hands of Russell & Sturgis, who are also proprietors of the Hotel Nantasket, — the most effective in its architecture of any of the great houses here. Its towers and pinnacles are numbered by the score, and it has the broadest of piazzas. In front of the hotel, toward the water, is the band-stand from which Reeve's celebrated band gives two concerts daily during the season, their entrancing music mingling with the monotone of the surf, to the delight of large audiences which assemble on the piazzas.

The Rockland Café, also under the same management, is joined to the hotel by a long arcade, and enjoys an excellent reputation for its chowders and fish dinners.

The Atlantic House, which crowns the hill of the same name, is a spacious and elegant hotel, always filled during the season with guests, including many of the representatives of wealth and culture in the metropolis. The view from here is very grand, commanding the entire beach and a vast expanse of the sea. The proprietors are L. Damon & Sons.

Bathing is, naturally enough, a prominent feature of Nantasket's attractions. Bath-houses are scattered all along the beach, where one may, for a small sum, — fifty to two-hundred per cent. of its value, — obtain the use of a suit for as long a time as he or she may choose to buffet the waves of the briny Atlantic. The most appreciative patrons of the surf seem to be the children, who are always ready to pull off shoes and stockings, and, armed with a wooden pail and shovel, amuse themselves with digging sand, and letting the surf break over their feet. It is very evident that not a few older people envy the children in this innocent amusement.

It is said that the life of the hotels and the drift of excursionists, great as they appear, are falling into the background, while the popularity of cottage life is rapidly on the increase. This plan is much more economical than boarding at the highest-price hotels, although those who have ample means find a summer spent at either the houses of Russell & Sturgis, or at the hostelry of Damon & Sons, most eminently satisfactory in every respect. New cottages spring up like mushrooms every year from one end of the beach to the other, and they represent every style of architecture, although Queen Anne is held responsible for the most frequent style as yet. But in size, coloring, and expense the cottages vary as widely as the tastes and wealth of their several owners. " There are big houses and little ; houses like the Chinese pagodas in old Canton blue-ware ; houses like castles, with towers and battlements ; houses like nests, and houses like barracks ; houses with seven gables, and houses with none at all."

During the heavy easterly gales of winter seaweed and kelp are washed ashore in great quantities. This is carted off by the farmers, who find it valuable as a fertilizer, and they are indebted to the sea for thousands of dollars' worth of this product every year. Nantasket in winter presents a gloomy contrast to its life and gayety in the summer. The winds are cold and fierce. The pretty cottages are deserted, and the sea moans with a sound betokening peril to the craft that ventures to tempt the waves. The nearly buried timbers of old vessels that are seen in the sands are relics of disaster in years gone by.

But in the summer months, Nantasket must ever remain a sea-side paradise to those who know its attractions.

IDLENESS.

By Sidney Harrison.

A FLUTTER 'mid the branches, and my heart
  Leaps with the life in that full chirp that breathes;
The brown, full-breasted sparrow with a dart
  Is at my feet amid the swaying wreaths
Of grass and clover; trooping blackbirds come
  With haughty step; the oriole, wren and jay
  Revel amid the cool, green moss in play,
Then off in clouds of music; while the drum
Of scarlet-crested woodpecker from yon '
Old Druid-haunting oak sends toppling down
A ruined memory of ages past;
O life and death — how blended to the last!

THE GRIMKÉ SISTERS.

THE FIRST AMERICAN WOMEN ADVOCATES OF ABOLITION AND WOMAN'S RIGHTS.

By George Lowell Austin.

THIS is an era of recollections. The events of twenty and twenty-five years ago are being read and reconsidered anew with as much interest as though they were the fresh and important events of the present. It was long claimed by those who believed that they thought and wrote with authority that not only was slavery the main cause of the civil war in America, but that the abolition of slavery was its chiefest object. A more sober criticism of the motives and deeds of those who were the prime actors in that inglorious struggle has tended somewhat to alter this opinion. It will, however, be again called to mind by a forthcoming biography, — that of Sarah and Angelina Grimké, better known as " the Grimké Sisters." The task of preparing this biography was intrusted to Mrs. Catherine H. Birney, of Washington, who knew the sisters well, and who lived for several years under the same roof with them.

There need be no hesitation in saying this book is one of the most interesting and valuable contributions to the history of abolitionism ever published. From first to last, during that momentous struggle, the phrase "the Grimké Sisters" was familiar to everybody, and the part which they enacted in the struggle was no less familiar. Mr. Phillips often spoke of them in his public addresses; they were prominent members of the anti-slavery societies; they themselves frequently appeared before large audiences on public platforms. Indeed, no history of the great moral cause would be complete that was not, in large part, made up of their noble deeds; and no less valiantly did they contend for Woman's Rights.

SARAH and ANGELINA GRIMKÉ were born in Charleston, South Carolina; Sarah, Nov. 26, 1792; Angelina, Feb. 20, 1805. They were the daughters of the Hon. John Fauchereau Grimké, a colonel in the revolutionary war, and judge of the Supreme Court of South Carolina. His ancestors were German on the father's side, French on the mother's; the Fauchereau family having left France in consequence of the revocation of the Edict of Nantes in 1685.

Judge Grimké's position, character, and wealth placed his family among the leaders of the very exclusive society of Charleston. His children were accustomed to luxury and display, to the service of slaves, and to the indulgence of every selfish whim, although the father's practical common-sense led him to protest against the habits to which such indulgences naturally led. To Sarah he paid particular attention, and was often heard to declare that if she had been of the other sex she would have made the greatest jurist in the land.

Children are born without prejudice, and the young children of Southern planters never felt or made any difference between their white and colored playmates. So that there is nothing singular in the fact that Sarah Grimké early felt such an abhorrence of the whole institution of slavery that she was sure it was born in her.

When Sarah was twelve years old two important events occurred to interrupt the even tenor of her life. Her brother Thomas was sent off to Yale College, leaving her companionless; but a little sister, Angelina Emily, the last child of her parents, and the pet and darling of Sarah from the moment the light dawned upon her blue eyes, came to take his place. Sarah almost became a mother to this little one; whither she led, Angelina followed closely.

In 1818 Judge Grimké's health began to decline. So faithful did Sarah nurse him that when it was decided that he should go to Philadelphia, she was chosen to accompany him. This first visit to the North was the most important event of Sarah's life, for the influences and impressions there received gave some shape to her vague and wayward fancies, and showed her a gleam of the light beyond the tangled path which still stretched before her.

Her father died; and in the vessel which carried his remains from Philadelphia Sarah met a party of Friends. She talked with them on religious matters, and after a few months acknowledged to one of them, in the course of a correspondence, her entire conversion to Quakerism. Ere long circumstances and the inharmonious life in her family urged her again to seek

Philadelphia, where she arrived in May, 1821. Angelina remained at Charleston, where she grew up a gay, fashionable girl.

We pass over the interesting correspondence which, from this time onward, was carried on between the sisters.

The strong contrast between Sarah and Angelina Grimké was shown not only in their religious feelings, but in their manner of treating the ordinary concerns of life, and in carrying out their convictions of duty. In her humility, and in her strong reliance on the " inner light," Sarah refused to trust her own judgment, even in the merest trifles, such as the lending of a book to a friend, postponing the writing of a letter, or sweeping a room to-day when it might be better to defer it until to-morrow. She says of this : " Perhaps to some, who have been led by higher ways than I have been into a knowledge of the truth, it may appear foolish to think of seeking direction in little things, but my mind has for a long time been in a state in which I have often felt a fear how I came in or went out, and I have found it a precious thing to stop and consult the mind of truth, and be governed thereby."

Already the sisters had begun to reflect upon the evils of slavery. Evidences of the tenor of their reflection are furnished in their letter, and also in Sarah's diary, which she commenced in 1828. Angelina was the first to express her abhorrence of the whole system ; while Sarah's mind, for a while at least, was too much absorbed by her disappointed hopes and her trials in the ministry to allow her to do much more than express sympathy with Angelina's anti-slavery sentiments.

In the autumn of 1829 Angelina left Charleston never to return, and made her home with Sarah in the home of Catherine Morris. She soon became interested in Quakerism, and eventually joined the Society. The daily records of their lives and thoughts, for the ensuing four or five years, exhibit them in the enjoyment of their quiet home, visiting prisons, hospitals, and almshouses, and mourning over no sorrow or sins but their own. Angelina was leading a life of benevolent effort, too busy to admit of the pleasure of society, and her Quaker associations did not favor contact with the world's people, or promote knowledge of the active movements in the larger reforms of the day. As to Sarah, she was suffering keenly under a great sorrow of her life.

Meanwhile, events were making ; the anti-slavery question was being agitated and discussed. In February, 1831, occurred the famous debate at Lane Seminary, near Cincinnati, presided over by Dr. Lyman Beecher. The eloquence of that debate swept over the country ; it flooded many hearts, and set souls aflame. Sarah Grimké also thought a *little*. Under date of " 5th mo., 12th, 1835," appears the following in Angelina's diary : —

Five months have elapsed since I wrote in this diary, since which time I have become deeply interested in the subject of abolition. I had long regarded this cause as utterly hopeless, but since I have examined anti-slavery principles, I find them so full of the power of truth, that I am confident not many years will roll by before the horrible traffic in human beings will be destroyed in this land of Gospel privileges. My soul has measurably stood in the stead of the poor slave, and my earnest prayers have been poured out that the Lord would be pleased to permit me to be instrumental of good to these degraded, oppressed, and suffering fellow-creatures. Truly, I often feel ready to go to prison or to death in this cause of justice, mercy, and love; and I do fully believe if I am called to return to Carolina, it will not be long before I shall suffer persecution of some kind or other.

When, after the Garrison riot, Mr. Garrison issued his appeal to the citizens of Boston, Angelina's anti-slavery enthusiasm was fully aroused. On the 30th of March of that year (1835) she wrote a letter to Mr. Garrison, — as *brave* a letter as was ever penned by the hand of woman. In it occur these thrilling words : —

If, she says, persecution is the means which God has ordained for the accomplishment of this great end, *Emancipation*, then, in dependence upon him for strength to bear it, I feel as if I could say, *Let It Come!* for it is my deep, solemn, deliberate conviction that *this is a cause worth dying for.* I say so from what I have seen, heard, and known in a land of slavery, where rests the darkness of Egypt, and where is found the sin of Sodom. Yes! *Let it come — let us suffer*, rather than insurrections should arise.

Mr. Garrison published the letter in the " Liberator " to the surprise of Angelina and the great displeasure and grief of her Quaker friends, and of her sister, Sarah, as well. But Angelina was not dismayed. In 1836 she wrote her " Appeal to Southern Women," and sent it to New York, where it was published as a pamphlet of thirty-six pages. Mr. Elizur Wright spoke of it, at the time, as " a patch of blue sky breaking through the storm-cloud of public indignation which had gathered so black over the handful of anti-slavery workers." The praise was not exaggerated. The pamphlet produced the most profound sensation wherever it was read.

Soon after its publication the sisters went to New York and there openly identified themselves with the members of the American Anti-Slavery Society; and also of the Female Anti-Slavery Society. The account of the first assembly of women, not Quakers, in a public place in America, addressed by American women, as given in these pages, is deeply interesting and touching from its very simplicity. We, who are so accustomed to hear women speak to promiscuous audiences on any and every subject, will naturally smile at the following memoranda by Angelina : —

We went home to tea with Julia Tappan, and Brother Weld was all anxiety to hear about the meeting. Julia undertook to give some account, and among other things mentioned that a warm-hearted abolitionist had found his way into the back part of the meeting, and was escorted out by Henry Ludlow. Weld's noble countenance instantly lighted up, and he exclaimed: " How supremely ridiculous to think of a man's being shouldered out of a meeting for fear he should hear a woman speak!" . . .

In the evening a colonizationist of this city came to introduce an abolitionist to Lewis Tappan. We women soon hedged in our expatriation brother, and held a long and interesting argument with him until near ten o'clock. He gave up so much that I could not see what he had to stand on when we left him.

After closing their meetings in New York the sisters held similar ones in New Jersey, all of which were attended only by women. From thence they went up the North River with Gerrit Smith, holding audiences at Hudson and Poughkeepsie. At the latter place they spoke to an assembly of colored people of both sexes, and this was the first time Angelina ever addressed a mixed audience.

The woman's rights agitation, while entirely separate from abolitionism, owes its origin to the interest this subject excited in the hearts and minds of American women; and to Sarah and Angelina Grimké must be accorded the credit of first making the woman question one of reform. They wrote and spoke often on the theme. Public feeling grew strong against them, and at last the Congregational ministers of Massachusetts saw proper to pass a resolution of censure against the sisters! This resolution was issued as a "Pastoral Letter," which, in the light and freedom of the present day, must be regarded as a most extraordinary document.

Whittier's muse found the "Pastoral Letter" a fitting theme for its vigorous, sympathetic utterances. The poem thus inspired is perhaps one of the very best among his many songs of freedom. It will be remembered as beginning thus :—

> "So this is all! the utmost reach
> Of priestly power the mind to fetter,
> When laymen *think*, when women *preach*,
> A war of words, a ' Pastoral Letter!' "

Up to this time nothing had been said by either of the sisters in their lectures concerning their views about women. They had carefully confined themselves to the subject of slavery, and the attendant topics of immediate emancipation, abstinence from the use of slave products, the errors of the Colonization Society, and the sin of prejudice on the account of color. But now that they had found their own rights invaded, they began to feel it was time to look out for the rights of their whole sex.

In the face of all this censure and ridicule the two sisters continued in the discharge of a duty to which they increasingly felt they were called from on high.

One is compelled, in this brief *résumé*, to hurry over much that is interesting and important. While the good work goes on we see the sisters everywhere faithful to their sense of duty, unflinching to all assailants.

In February, 1838, Sarah Grimké spoke for the last time in public, and in the month of May following, Angelina was united in marriage to Theodore D. Weld. "No marriage," says Mrs. Birney, "could have been more fitting in every respect. The solemn relation was never entered upon in more holiness of purpose or in higher resolve to hold themselves strictly to the best they were capable of. It was a rededication of lives long consecrated to God and humanity; of souls knowing no selfish ambition, seeking before all things the glory of their Creator in the elevation of his creatures everywhere. The entire unity of spirit in which they afterwards lived and labored, the tender affection which, through a companionship of more than forty years, knew no diminution, made a family life so perfect and beautiful that it brightened and inspired all who were favored to witness it. No one could be with them under the most ordinary circumstances without feeling the force and influence of their characters."

The happy couple settled down for their first house-keeping at Fort Lee, on the Hudson. They were scarcely settled amid their new surroundings before the sisters received a formal notice of their disownment by the Society of Friends because of Angelina's marriage. In December, 1839, the happiness of the little household was increased by the birth of a son, who received the name of Charles Stuart, in loving remembrance of the eminent English philanthropist, with whom Mr. Weld had been as a brother, and whom he regarded as living as near the angels as mortal man could live.

In the latter part of February, 1840, Mr. Weld, having purchased a farm of fifty acres at Belleville, New Jersey, removed his family there. The visitors to the Belleville farm — chiefly old and new anti-slavery friends — were numerous, and were always received with a cordiality which left no room to doubt its sincerity.

In many ways the members of this united household were diligent in good works. If a neighbor required a few hundred dollars, to save the fore-closure of a mortgage, the combined resources of the family were taxed to aid him ; if a poor student needed a helping hand in his preparation for college, or for teaching, it was gladly extended to him, — perhaps his board and lodging given him for six months or a year, — with much valuable instruction thrown in. The instances of charity of this kind were many, and were performed with such a cheerful spirit that Sarah only incidentally alludes to the increase of their cares and work at such times. In fact, their roof was ever a shelter for the homeless, a home for the friendless ; and it is pleasant to record that the return of ingratitude, so often made for benevolence of this kind, was never their portion. They always seem to have had the sweet satisfaction of knowing, sooner or later, that their kindness was not thrown away or under-estimated.

In 1852 the Raritan Bay Association, consisting of thirty or forty educated and cultured families of congenial tastes, was formed at Eagleswood, near Perth Amboy, New Jersey ; and a year later Mr. and Mrs. Weld were invited to join the Association, and take charge of its educational department. They accepted, in the hope of finding in the change greater social advantages for themselves and their children, with less responsibility and less labor ; for of these last the husband, wife, and sister, in their Belleville School, had had more than they were physically able to endure longer. Their desire and plan was to establish, with the children of the residents at Eagleswood, a school also for others, and to charge such a moderate remuneration only as would enable the middle classes to profit by it. In this project, as with every other, no selfish ambition found a place. They removed to Eagleswood in the autumn of 1854.

In the new school Angelina taught history, for which she was admirably qualified, while Sarah taught French, and was also book-keeper.

It is scarcely necessary to say that few schools have ever been established upon such a basis of conscientiousness and love, and with such adaptability in its conductors, as that at Eagleswood ; few have ever held before the pupils so high a moral standard, or urged them on to such noble purposes in life. Children entered there spoiled by indulgence, selfish, uncontrolled, sometimes vicious. Their teachers studied them carefully ; confidence was gained, weaknesses sounded, elevation measured. Very slowly often, and with infinite patience and perseverance, but successfully in nearly every case, these children were redeemed. The idle became industrious, the selfish considerate, the disobedient and wayward repentant and gentle. Sometimes the fruits of all this labor and forbearance did not show themselves immediately, and, in a few instances, the seed sown did not ripen until the boy or girl had left school and mingled with the world. Then the contrast between the common, every-day aims they encountered, and the teachings of their Eagleswood mentors, was forced upon them. Forgotten lessons of truth and honesty and purity were remembered, and the wavering resolve was stayed and strengthened ; worldly expediency gave way before the magnanimous purpose, cringing subserviency before independent manliness.

Then came the war. In 1862 Mrs. Weld published one of the most powerful things she ever wrote. — "A Declaration of War on Slavery." We have not the space to follow the course of the sisters' lives farther ; and, were it otherwise, the events narrated would be all too familiar. Sarah, after a somewhat prolonged illness, died on the 23d of December, 1873, at Hyde Park, Mass. The funeral services were conducted by the Rev. Francis Williams, and eloquent remarks were made also by Wm. Lloyd Garrison. On the 26th of October, 1879, Angelina passed quietly away, and the last services were in keeping with the record of the life then commemorated. We close this writing with a passage from the remarks which Wendell Phillips made on that occasion. No words could possibly be more touching or more eloquent : —

When I think of Angelina there comes to me the picture of the spotless dove in the tempest, as she battles with the storm, seeking for some place to rest her foot. She reminds me of innocence personified in Spenser's poem. In her girlhood, alone, heart-led, she comforts the slave in his quarters, mentally struggling with the problems his position wakes her to. Alone, not confused, but seeking something to lean on, she grasps the Church, which proves a broken reed. No whit disheartened, she turns from one sect to another, trying each by the infallible touchstone of that clear, child-like conscience. The two old, lonely Quakers rest her foot awhile. But the eager soul must work, not rest in testimony. Coming North at last, she makes her own religion one of sacrifice and toil. Breaking away from, rising above, all forms, the dove floats at last in the blue sky where no clouds reach. . . . This is no place for tears. Graciously, in loving kindness and tenderly, God broke the shackles and freed her soul. It was not the dust which surrounded her that we loved. It was not the form which encompassed her that we revere; but it was the soul. We linger a very little while, her old comrades. The hour comes, it is even now at the door, that God will open our eyes to see her as she is : the white-souled child of twelve years old ministering to want and sorrow; the ripe life, full of great influences; the serene old age, example and inspiration whose light will not soon go out. Farewell for a very little while. God keep us fit to join thee in that broader service on which thou hast entered.

TEN DAYS IN NANTUCKET.

BY ELIZABETH PORTER GOULD. [1]

ONE night in the early part of July, 1883, as the successful real-estate broker, Mr. Gordon, returned to his home from his city office, his attention was arrested by a lively conversation between the members of his family on the wonders of Nantucket. The sound of this old name brought so vividly back to him his own boyish interest in the place, that almost before he was aware of it he announced his return home to his family by saying: "Well, supposing we go to Nantucket this summer? It is thirty-four miles from mainland, and so free from malaria there is no better place for fishing and sailing, and there would be a mental

EARLY MORNING, NANTUCKET.

interest in looking around the island which would be instructive and delightful, and, perhaps, profitable for me from a business point of view."

Mrs. Gordon, who had of late years developed a keen interest for the historic and antique, immediately seconded her husband in his suggestion; and before the evening closed a letter was sent to Nantucket asking for necessary information as to a boarding-place there, for at least ten days, for a party of five, — Mr. and Mrs. Gordon, their daughter Bessie, twenty years of age, their son Tom, fifteen years, and a favorite cousin of theirs, Miss Ray, who was then visiting them, and whose purse, as Mr. Gordon had so often practically remembered, was not equal to her desire to see and to know.

In a few days satisfactory arrangements were made, which ended in their all leaving the Old Colony depot, Boston, in the half-past twelve train, for Wood's Holl, where they arrived in two hours and a half. From that place they took the steamer for a nearly three hours' sail to Nantucket, only to stop for a few moments at Martha's Vineyard.

While they were thus ploughing their way on the mighty deep, Nantucket's famous crier, "Billy" Clark, had climbed to his position in the tower of the Unitarian church of the town, — as had been his daily custom for years, — spy-glass in hand, to see the steamer when she should come in sight. Between five and six o'clock, the repeated blowing of the horn from the tower announced to the people his success, and became the signal for them to make ready to receive those who should come to their shores. Just before seven o'clock the steamer arrived. While she was being fastened to the wharf, Tom was attracted by this same "Billy," who, having received the daily papers, was running up the wharf toward the town ringing his bell and crying out the number of passengers on board, and other important news, which Tom failed to hear in the noise of the crowd. A few minutes' walk brought the party to their boarding-place. When Mrs. Gordon spied the soft, crayon likeness of Benjamin Franklin on the wall, as she stepped into the house, her historical pulse quickened to such an extent that she then and there determined to hunt up more about the Folgers; for was not Benjamin Franklin's mother a Folger and born on this island? Then, as she saw about her some old portraits and copies of the masters, and, above all, a copy of Murillo's Immaculate Conception in the dining-room, she was sure that the atmosphere of her new quarters would be conducive to her happiness and growth. The others saw the pictures, but they appreciated more fully, just then, the delicious blue-fish which was on hand to appease their hunger.

After a night of restful sleep, such as Nantucket is noted for giving, they all arose early to greet a beautiful morning, which they used, partly, for a stroll around the town. Of course, they all registered at the Registry Agency on Orange street, where Mr. Godfrey, who had entertained them by his interesting guide-book on Nantucket, gave them a kind welcome. Then they walked along the Main street, noticing the bank, built in 1818, and passed some quaint old houses with their gables, roofs, and sides, all finished alike, which Burdette has described as "being shingled, shangled, shongled, and shungled." Tom was struck with the little railings which crowned so many of the houses; and which, since the old fishing days' prosperity did not call the people on the house-tops to watch anxiously for the expected ships, were now more ornamental than useful. They passed, at the corner of Ray's Court, a sycamore tree, the largest and oldest on the island, and soon halted at the neat Soldiers' Monument, so suggestive of the patriotic valor of the island people.

Later they found on Winter street the Coffin School-house, — a brick building with two white pillars in front and a white cupola, — which was back from the street, behind some shade trees, and surrounded by an iron fence. As they looked at it Miss Ray read aloud the words inscribed on the front: —

FOUNDED 1827 BY
ADMIRAL SIR ISAAC COFFIN, BART.
ERECTED
1852.

They were also interested to see, near by, a large white building, known as the High School-house. As they neared home Tom's eyes noticed the sign of a Nantucket birds' exhibition, and a visit to that place was made.

During the walk Mrs. Gordon had been particularly interested in the large cobble-stones which the uneven streets supported in addition to the green grass, and also the peculiar Nantucket cart, with its step behind.

On their return to their boarding-place, they joined a party that had been formed to go to the Cliff, a sandy bluff about a mile north from the town, where they were told was to be found the best still-water bathing on the island. Soon they were all on the yacht "Dauntless," which hourly plied between the two places; in twenty minutes they were landed at the Cliff; and fifteen minutes later they were all revelling in the warm, refreshing water. Bessie declared that in all her large bathing experience on the north shore she had never enjoyed anything like this. Miss Ray felt that here in this warm, still water was her opportunity to learn to swim; so she accepted the kind teaching of a friend; but, alas, her efforts savored more of hard work to plough up the Atlantic ocean than of an easy, delightful pleasure bottling up knowledge for some possible future use. While Miss Ray was thus struggling with the ocean, and Bessie and Tom were sporting like two fish, — for both were at home in the water, — Mr. Gordon was looking around the Cliff with his business eye wide open. As he walked along the road back from the shore, and saw the fine views which it afforded him, he admired the judgment of Eastman Johnson, the artist, in building his summer-house and studio there. A little farther on, upon the Bluffs, the highest point on the island, he noted the house of Charles O'Conor with the little brick building close by for his library; he then decided that an island which could give such physical benefit as this was said to have given to Mr. O'Conor, would not be a bad one in which to invest. So the value of the Cliff or Bluffs he placed in his note-book for future use.

At the same time that Mr. Gordon was exploring the land Mrs. Gordon was in the office of two gallant young civil engineers, exploring the harbor! In fact she was studying a map of the surroundings of the harbor, which these young men had made to aid them in their work of

building a jetty from Brant Point to the bell-buoy. As she examined it
she found it hard to believe that Nantucket had ever stood next to Boston

VIEWS IN NANTUCKET, MASS.

and Salem, as the third commercial town in the Commonwealth. She
sympathized deeply with the people of the years gone by who had been

obliged to struggle with such a looking harbor as the map revealed, and
said that she should go home to learn more of the "Camels," which
she honored more than ever. When they told her that probably three
years more than the two that had been given to the work were needed
to finish the jetty, and that there was a slight possibility that another one
would be needed for the best improvement of the harbor, she thought
her interest in the matter could be better kept alive if she should hunt
up her old trigonometry and learn that all over again! With this idea
she left the young men, whose kindness to her she fully appreciated, and
went to find her party. She soon found, on the yacht ready to go back
to town, all but Miss Ray; she had chosen to take one of the many carriages which she had noticed were constantly taking passengers back and
forth from the town to the Cliff, at the rate of ten cents apiece.

Later in the afternoon their attention was arrested by another one of
the town-criers, — Tom had learned that there were three in the town, —
who was crying out that a meat-auction would be held that night at half-
past six o'clock. When they were told that these meat-auctions had
been the custom of the town for years, they were anxious to attend one; but
another engagement at that hour prevented their so doing, much to
Tom's regret.

The next day was Sunday. As Bessie and Tom were anxious to see
all of the nine churches of which they had read, they were, at first, in
doubt where to go; whereas their mother had no questions whatever,
since she had settled in her own mind, after having reduced all sects
to the Episcopal and the Roman Catholic, that the Episcopal Church
was the true historic one, and, therefore, the only one for her personal
interest, that she should go to the St. Paul's on Fair street. Mr. Gordon
usually went to church with his wife, although he often felt that the simplicity of the early apostolic days was found more in the Congregational
form of worship. This day he yielded to Tom's desire to go to
the square-steepled Congregational Church on Centre street, to hear
Miss Baker, who had been preaching to the congregation for three
years. He entered the church with some prejudice; but soon he became
so much interested in the good sermon that he really forgot that the
preacher was a woman! Miss Ray and Bessie went to the Unitarian
Church on Orange street, to which the beautiful-toned Spanish bell invited them. After an interesting service, on their way out they met
Tom, who wished to look into the pillared church of the Methodists,
near the bank, and also into the "Ave Maria" on Federal street,
where the Roman Catholics worshipped. Miss Ray, being anxious
to attend a Friends' meeting in their little meeting-house on Fair street,
decided to do so the following Sunday, if she were in town; while Bessie said that she should hunt up then the two Baptist churches, the one on
Summer street and the other, particularly for the colored people, on
Pleasant street. Their surprise that a town of a little less than four thousand inhabitants should contain so many churches was modified some-

what when they remembered that once, in 1840, the number of inhabitants was nearly ten thousand.

In the afternoon the party visited some of the burying-grounds of the town, six of which were now in use. The sight of so many unnamed graves in the Friends' cemetery, at the head of Main street, saddened Miss Ray; and she was glad to see the neat little slabs which of late years had marked the graves of their departed ones. They strolled around the Prospect Hill, or Unitarian Cemetery, near by, and wished to go into the Catholic one on the same street; but, as Mrs. Gordon was anxious to see some of the old headstones and epitaphs in the North burying-ground on North Liberty street, and their time was limited, they went there instead. When Tom saw her delight as she read on the old stones the date of 1770, 1772, and some even earlier, he said that she must go out to the ancient burial-ground on the hill near the water-works and see the grave of John Gardner, Esq., who was buried there in 1706. As he said this one of the public carriages happened to be within sight, and she proposed that they take it and go immediately to that sacred spot. When they arrived there her historic imagination knew no bounds; her soliloquy partook of the sentiment — in kind only, not in degree — which inspired Mark Twain when he wept over the grave of Adam. In the mean while, Mr. Gordon had gone to the Wannacomet Waterworks, which supplied the town with pure water from the old Washington-pond. He there noted in his note-book that this important movement in the town's welfare was another reason why investment in the island would be desirable.

As they started to go back to town from the burial-ground Tom wished that they could drive to the south-west suburbs, to see the South and also the colored burying-grounds, for he should feel better satisfied if he could see everything of a kind that there was! But Mrs. Gordon had seen enough for one day, and so they drove to their boarding-house instead.

The ringing of the sweet-toned church bell the next morning at seven o'clock reminded Miss Ray of her desire to visit the tower which contained it. She had noticed how it rang out three times during the day, at seven, twelve, and nine o'clock, and, for the quiet Nantucket town, she hoped that the old custom would never be dropped. And then this bell had a peculiar attraction for her, for it was like the one which was on her own church in Boston, the New Old South. She had been greatly interested in reading that this "Old Spanish Bell," as it was called, was brought from Lisbon in 1812; that it was stored in a cellar for three years, when it was bought by subscription for about five hundred dollars, and put in this tower. She had read, further, in Godfrey's guide-book, that "some little time after the bell had been in use, the sound of its mellow tones had reached the Hub; and so bewitching were the musical vibrations of this queenly bell (e) of Nantucket to many of the good people of the renowned 'City of Notions,' that the agents of the Old South Church negotiated with the agents of the Unitarian Church, saying that they had a very fine clock in their tower; that they had been so unfortunate as to have their bell broken, and wished to know at what price this bell could be procured. The agents of the Unitarian Church replied that they had a very fine bell in their tower, and would like to know at what price the Old South Society would sell their clock. The bell weighs one thousand five hundred and seventy-five pounds; the Boston gentlemen offered one dollar a pound for it, and upon finding they could not get it at any price, they asked where it came from; and having ascertained its history, sent to Lisbon to the same foundry and procured that which they now have." And she had been told further that this same bell had been removed to the new church on the Back Bay. With all this pleasant association with the bell of her own church, of course she must pay it a visit. So at about nine o'clock, after Mr. Gordon and Tom had gone off with two gentlemen for a day's blue-fishing, she, with Mrs. Gordon and Bessie, started out for their morning's sight-seeing. In a half hour's time they had climbed the stairs to the tower, and were admiring the fine new clock, — a gift from one of Nantucket's sons, now living in New York, — which had been first set in motion two years before, to replace an old one which had told the time for over half a century. A little farther up they saw the famous bell, and Miss Ray did wish that she could read Spanish so as to translate the inscription which was upon it. A few steps more brought them into the dome itself. Here, then, was the place where "Billy" came to sight the steamers; and here was where a watchman stayed every night to watch for fires. Whenever he saw one, Bessie said his duty was to hang a lantern upon a hook in the direction of the fire and give the alarm. She said that this had been the custom for years. As they were all enjoying this finest view which the island affords, Bessie spied the Old Mill in the distance, and as she had that painted on a shell as a souvenir of her Nantucket trip she must surely visit it. So they were soon wending their way up Orange street, through Lyons to Pleasant, and then up South Mill to the Old Mill itself. On paying five cents apiece, they were privileged to go to the top and look through the spy-glass, and also see the miller grind some corn. This old windmill, built in 1746, with its old oaken beams still strong and sound, situated on a hill by itself, was to Bessie the most picturesque thing that she had seen. She associated this with the oldest house on the island, built in 1686, facing the south, which she had seen the day before.

In the afternoon they continued their sight-seeing by visiting the Athenæum on Federal street. They found it to be a large white building with pillars in front, on the lower floor of which Miss Ray was particularly pleased to see such a good library of six thousand volumes, and a reading-room with the leading English and American periodicals, the use of which she learned was to be gained by the payment of a small sum. Bessie was attracted to the oil-painting on the wall of Abraham Quary, who was the last of the Indian race on the island. Then they examined, in an adjoining room, the curiosities gathered together for public inspection. Here they found the model of the "Camels," and also the jaw of a sperm whale, seventeen feet long, with forty-six teeth and a weight of eight hundred pounds. Bessie said that the whale from which it was taken was eighty-seven feet long and weighed two hundred tons. When Mrs. Gordon learned that this very whale was taken in the Pacific Ocean and brought to the Island by a Nantucket Captain, she became as much interested in it as in the "Camels," for surely it had an historical interest. After an hour spent in this entertaining manner, they returned to their boarding-place in time to greet the gentlemen who had come back with glowing accounts of their day's work, or rather pleasure, for they had met with splendid success. Tom's fingers were blistered, but what was that compared to the fun of blue-fishing!

What particularly interested the ladies was a "Portuguese man of war" which one of the gentlemen had caught in a pail and brought home alive. This beautiful specimen of a fish, seen only at Nantucket, their hostess said, and seldom caught alive, was admired by all, who, indeed, were mostly ignorant of the habits or even the existence of such a creature. Bessie wondered how such a lovely iridescent thing could be poison to the touch. Tom promised to study up about it when he should begin his winter studies, whereupon his mother said that if he would tell her what he should learn about it she would write it out for the benefit of them all.

The next morning they all started from the wharf at nine o'clock in the miniature steamer, "Island Belle," for Wauwinet, a place seven miles from the town. Miss Ray had become interested in the pretty Indian names which she had heard, and was struck with this, which she learned was the name of an old Indian chief who once controlled a large eastern part of the island. In an hour they landed on the beach at Wauwinet. They found it decorated with its rows of scallop-shells, some of which they gathered as they walked along. Some of the party made use of this still-water bathing, while others ran across the island, some three hundred yards, to enjoy the surf-bathing there. Tom was delighted with this novelty of two beaches, separated by such a narrow strip of land, that he was continually going back and forth to try the water in both places. He only wished that he could go up a little farther where he had been told the land was only one hundred yards wide, — the narrowest part of the island. After a shore dinner at the Wauwinet House, and another stroll on the beaches, they started for the town on the yacht "Lilian," which twice a day went back and forth. The wind was unfavorable, so they were obliged to go fourteen miles instead of seven, thus using two hours instead of one for the sail. On their way they passed the places known as Polpis, Quidnet, and Coatue. Mr. Gordon was so much impressed with the advantages of Coatue that he noted the fact in his note-book; while his wife became so much interested in the nautical expressions used that she declared that she should get Bowditch's "Navigation," and see if she could find those terms in it; she must know more of navigation than

she did.   As they landed at the wharf they heard "Billy" Clarke crying out
that the New Bedford band would give a grand concert at Surf Side the
next day.   Now, as this kind of music had been the chief thing which they
had missed among the pleasures of Nantucket, of course they must go
and hear it.   So the next afternoon, at two o'clock, they were on the cars
of the narrow-gauge railroad, bound for the Surf-Side Hotel, which they
reached in fifteen minutes, passing on the way a station of the life-saving
service department.   They spent an hour or two seated on the bluff overlooking the grand surf-beach, and enjoying the strains of music as they
came from the hotel behind them.   It must be confessed that Mr. Gordon
was so interested in noting the characteristics of this part of the island with
an eye to business, that he did not lose himself either in the music of
the band or the ocean.   On his way back to town, when he expressed his
desire to build a cottage for himself on that very spot, Surf Side, Mrs.
Gordon would not assent to any such proposition; for she had settled in
her own mind that there was no place like Brant Point, where she
and Bessie had been that forenoon; for did not the keeper of the light-
house there tell her, when she was at the top of it, that on that spot was
built the first light-house in the United States, in 1746?   That was enough
for her, surely.   The matter was still under discussion when Miss Ray
told them to wait until they had visited 'Sconset before they should
decide the question.   As for her she could scarcely wait for the next morning to come when they should go there.   And when it did come it
found her, at half-past eight o'clock, decorating with pond-lilies, in honor
of the occasion, the comfortable excursion-wagon, capable of holding their
party of eight besides the driver.   By nine o'clock they were driving up
Orange street by the Sherburne and Bay View Houses, on their way to
Siasconset, or, 'Sconset, as it is familiarly called.

As they passed a large white building known as the Poor Farm,
Tom was surprised that a town noted for its thrift and temperance should
be obliged to have such an institution.   Bessie was glad to learn that they
were going over the old road instead of the new one, while Miss Ray
would rather have gone over the new one, so as to have seen the mile-
stones which Dr. Ewer, of New York, had put up by the wayside.
They met the well-known Captain Baxter, in his quaint conveyance,
making his daily trip to the town from 'Sconset.   As they rode for
miles over the grassy moors with no trees or houses in sight, none of them
could believe that the island had once been mostly covered with beautiful
oak trees.   Soon the village, with its quaint little houses built close together on the narrow streets, which wound around in any direction to
find the town-pump, its queer, one-story school-house, its post-office,
guarded by the gayly-colored "Goddess of Liberty," was before, or
rather all around them.   They had all enjoyed their ride of seven and a
half miles; and now, on alighting from the carriage, the party separated
in different directions.   Miss Ray insisted upon bathing in the surf-
beach here in spite of its coarse sand and rope limitations, since it was the

farthest out in the Atlantic Ocean. Her experience with the strong undertow in its effects upon herself and upon those who watched her is one, which, as no words can portray it, Tom has decided to draw out for some future Puck ; for he thinks that it is too good to be lost to the public.

Mrs. Gordon and Bessie walked among the houses, noticing the peculiar names which adorned some of them, and, indeed, going inside one of the oldest where a step-ladder was used for the boys of the household to get up into their little room. They crossed the bridge which led them to the Sunset Heights where some new houses, in keeping with the style of the old ones, were being built. They were pleased to see this unity of design, rather than the modern cottage which had intruded itself upon that coast. In their walk they learned that about eleven or twelve families spent the winter at 'Sconset. The air was intensely invigorating, so much so that Mrs. Gordon, who was no walker at home, was surprised at herself with what she was doing without fatigue. Later they found Mr. Gordon looking at the new church which had just been completed, and which he had ascertained was built for no sectarian purpose, but for the preaching of the truth. They all met at noon for their lunch, after which they went a mile and a half farther to visit the Sankaty Head light-house, the best one of the five on the island. The keeper kindly escorted them up the fifty-six steps to the top, where they learned that the point of the light was one hundred and sixty-five feet above the level of the sea. He gave them some more facts relative to the light, interspersed with personal experiences. Tom said that he should remember particularly the fact that he told him that this light-house would be the first one that he should see whenever he should come home from a European trip.

Two hours later they were relating their pleasant experiences in the dining-room of their boarding-house, while enjoying the delicious blue-fish which gratified their hunger. As for Miss Ray her anticipations had been realized ; and that night she wrote to a certain young man in Boston that she knew of no place in America where they could be more by themselves and away from the world, when their happy time should come in the following summer, than at 'Sconset.

The next afternoon found them all listening to Mrs. McCleave, as she faithfully exhibited the many interesting curiosities of her museum, in her home on Main street. Mrs. Gordon was very much interested in the Cedar Vase, so rich with its "pleasant associations," while Bessie was delighted with the beautiful carved ivory, with its romantic story as told by its owner. Miss Ray considered Mrs. McCleave, with her benevolent face, her good ancestry, and her eager desire to learn and impart, a good specimen of the well-preserved Nantucket woman.

Through the courtesy of their hostess they were privileged, on their way back, to visit the house of Miss Coleman, on Centre street, there to see the wonderful wax figure of a baby six months old, said to be the likeness of the Dauphin of France, the unfortunate son of Louis XVI.

When Mrs. Gordon learned that this was brought to Nantucket in 1786, by one of her own sea-captains, she became very much excited over it. As she realized then that her knowledge of French history was too meagre to fully understand its historical import, although she appreciated its artistic value, she determined that another winter should be partially devoted to that study. So she added " French history " to " Camels," " Light-houses," " Navigation," and " Indians," which were already in her note-book. She had added " Indians " the day before when her interest in them had been quickened by some accounts of the civilization of the early Indians in Nantucket, which seemed to her almost unprecedented in American history. After supper Mr. and Mrs. Gordon went out in a row-boat to enjoy the moonlight evening, Tom went to the skating-rink, Miss Ray spent the evening with some friends at the Ocean House near by, while Bessie went out for a moonlight sail with some friends from a western city, whom, she said, she had " discovered, not made." Her appreciation of a fine rendering of her favorite Raff Cavatina by a talented young gentleman of the party, soon after her arrival, had been the means of bringing together these two souls on the musical heights, which afterwards had led to an introduction to the other members of the party, all of whom she had enjoyed during the week that had passed. And now, with these newly-found friends, on this perfect July evening, with its full moon and fresh south-westerly breeze, in the new yacht " Lucile," she found perfect enjoyment. Pleasant stories were related, and one fish-story was allowed, to give spice to the occasion. After a little more than two hours' sail they found themselves returning to the Nantucket town, which, in the moonlight, presented a pretty appearance.

The next day, Saturday, Mr. Gordon and Tom started early to sail around the island, with an intention of landing on the adjoining island, Tuckernuck. Tom had calculated that it would be quite a sail, for he knew that Nantucket Island was fourteen miles long, and averaged four miles in width; and his father had decided that such a trip would give him a better idea of the island's best points for building purposes. On their return at night they found that the ladies had spent a pleasant day, bathing, riding, and visiting some Boston friends who were stopping at the Springfield House, a short distance from them. Bessie had found more pleasure in the company of the young musician and his friends, having attended one of the morning *musicales* which they were accustomed to have by themselves in the hall of the Athenæum. Tom and his father had much to tell of their day's pleasure.

Mr. Gordon, for once in his life, felt the longing which he knew had so often possessed his wife, to go back and live in the years gone by; for if he could now transfer himself to the year 1659, he might buy this whole island of Thomas Mayhew for thirty pounds and two beaver hats. What a lost opportunity for a good business investment! As it was, however, some valuable notes were added to his note-book, suggested by the trip, which time alone will give to the world. He was more and more convinced that the future well-being of Nantucket was more in the hands of real-estate brokers and summer pleasure-seekers, than in those of the manufacturers, agriculturists, or even the fishing men as of old. He could see no other future for her, and he should work accordingly. His chief regret was that the island was so barren of trees.

They spent the next day, Sunday, in attending church, as they had planned, and in pleasant conversation and rest preparatory to their departure for Boston on the following morning. They expressed gratitude that they had not been prevented by sickness or by one rainy day from carrying out all the plans which had been laid for the ten days. Mrs. Gordon very much regretted that they had not seen the famous Folger clock which was to be seen at the house of a descendant of Walter Folger, the maker of it. She should certainly see it the first thing, if she ever were in Nantucket again; for she considered the man, who, unaided, could make such a clock, the greatest mechanical genius that ever lived. She felt this still more when she was told that the clock could not be mended until there could be found a mechanic who was also an astronomer.

At seven o'clock the next morning they were all on board the steamer, as she left the old town of Nantucket in the distance. Mrs. Gordon looked longingly back at Brant Point, which she still felt was the best spot on the island; while Bessie eagerly watched for the little flag which a certain young gentleman was yet waving from the wharf.

At half-past one they were in Boston, and an hour later at their suburban home, all delighted with their short stay in Nantucket. They felt that they had seen about all that there was to be seen there, and they were glad to have visited the island before it should be clothed with more modern garments.

A BIRTHDAY SONNET.

By George W. Bungay.

Our days are like swift shuttles in the loom,
In which time weaves the warp and woof of fate;
Its varied threads that interpenetrate
The pattern woven, picture bride and groom,
A life-like scene in their own happy home.
There are some frayed and shaded strands, fair Kate,
But lines of purest gold illuminate
Our wedded lot, as stars the heavenly dome.
And come what may, sunshine or chilling rain,
Prosperity and peace or woe instead,
Untruth and selfishness shall never stain
The web of love and hope illustrated.
Not even death unravels when we die,
The woven work approved of God on high.

ELIZABETH.[1]

A ROMANCE OF COLONIAL DAYS.

By Frances C. Sparhawk, Author of " A Lazy Man's Work."

CHAPTER XX.

GREEK MEETS GREEK.

It was two weeks after the scene at Colonel Archdale's dinner-party. There was quite a knot of people in Madam Pepperell's drawing-room. All the household at Seascape had come on the way home from a drive to pay a morning visit here, and found the in-door coolness refreshing. Colonel Archdale, who had joined his son, was there also. Mr. Royal, as it happened, was in Portsmouth that morning.

Edmonson had been exemplary enough in avoiding the cant of pretended regret for what must have given him pleasure. Archdale had no complaints to make on that score, but he distrusted Edmonson more and more, and perceived more clearly that he was attracted by Elizabeth. He wondered if she encouraged him: that was not like the person she seemed to be; yet why not? She had assured Archdale more than once that she was free, and her certainty had given him comfort. But he was here this morning for another purpose than to weigh the question of Miss Royal's fancy. If she did encourage Edmonson she was all the more inexplicable.

Stephen bent over Lady Dacre's chair, talking gayly to her; yet his eyes wandered every now and then, and, gradually, after he had stopped several times beside one and another, he came up to Elizabeth, as she was sitting listening to a young lady who, with her brother, had come back from town with Madam Pepperell, the night before, to spend a few days at the house.

As Stephen stood behind her chair he looked across the room, and saw Edmonson leaning with folded arms against a window. The light fell over his face; he had been looking at Elizabeth, but his eyes met Archdale's at once with an expression meant for cool scrutiny and a dash of insolent triumph at the victory he had scored. Edmonson's fierceness was not easily fettered; the dark shadow in his heart darted over his face, and, withdrawing as hastily, left to view a light that blazed in his eyes and only slowly died down into the cordial warmth necessary between guest and host, even under peculiar circumstances. Stephen's face darkened also, but his feeling was less, and his control greater. Elizabeth was listening quietly to some account of a merry-making at

[1] Copyright, 1884, by Frances C. Sparhawk.

which Katie must have been present, for her name occurred frequently in the narrative. As she perceived that Archdale was behind her she looked round at him a moment, and by a few words included him in the conversation. She was as entertaining as usual and rather more talkative after he came. Yet he thought that under her ease of manner he detected a current of nervousness that made him the more anxious to carry out the purpose with which he had come to her.

But it was not easy to find any excuse for withdrawing her from the circle in which she had made herself so welcome. At last, however, under cover of a general movement, which he had secretly instigated, he succeeded in getting her into the library, on the plea of a message to her father. When there, he closed the door behind him, and said : —

"I have a message to your father, it is true, Mistress Royal, but it is only to beg him to interfere."

"Interfere?" she echoed with a nervousness that this time was unmistakable.

"Pray be seated," he said, drawing a chair toward her as she stood by the mantel.

"Thank you, but — I don't mind standing. What you — the business will not take long, you said."

"As you please." And he stood facing her on the opposite side of the great fireplace.

She heard his tones, glanced at him, and sat down. He took a chair also, still placing himself so that he could watch her. She grew plainly more nervous.

"Who is Mr. Hartly?" he asked, abruptly.

She looked at him in a frightened way, and the hand that she lifted to her throat was trembling.

"He is " — she began, then she stopped; without any warning her expression and her manner changed, for with the coming of what she had dreaded came the strength to meet it. There was no more tremulousness of voice or hand, and the face that looked at Stephen Archdale was the face of a woman who met him upon equal terms; yet, as he looked at her steadily, he was not quite sure even of that; it seemed to him that it would require an effort on his part to keep at her level; that at least he must stand at his full height. She sat silent, meeting his steady gaze. There was a dignity about her that would have been haughtiness but for her simplicity. Even her dress carried out the effect of this simplicity; it was a white muslin, very plain, and the single pink hollyhock that the new guest had slipped into her hair, and Elizabeth had forgotten, gave to her attire the touch of warmth that something in her face showed, too. It was to Stephen the calmness of flesh and blood, not of marble, that he was looking at; a possibility of life and motion was there, but a possibility beyond his reach. Some one might arouse her; to him she was impassive.

"You've not finished your sentence," he said, coldly.

"Why should I? You know the rest of it."

"Nevertheless, I wish you would say it."

"Very well. Mr. Hartly is an agent of Mr. Peterborough."

"And Mr. Peterborough?"

"My solicitor."

"You mean your father's?"

"Yes, and mine, too."

"Then you have property of your own?"

"Yes. You did not know it?"

"I heard of it yesterday. Your property is no concern of mine, you understand." She was silent. Under the circumstances the statement was significant. "Mr. Hartly came to my father the other day," he went on. Still no answer. "Possibly you knew it?" he persisted. She lifted her eyes which had been fixed on the cover of a book that her fingers were toying with, and said:—

"Yes."

Stephen waited to choose words which should not express too forcibly the impetuous feeling that shone in his eyes and rang in his voice when he spoke.

"Let me put a case to you," he said, "or, rather, not an indifferent case, but our own, and hear how it sounds in plain English. How we were married, if married we are, it is useless to speak of; how absolutely nothing we are to one another it is unnecessary also to say. I appreciate your efforts and your courtesy when I see so plainly that it is with difficulty you can bring yourself even to speak a word to me." Elizabeth glanced up a moment, and down again, and her fingers went on idly turning the leaves of the book. "When I see what social powers you have," he pursued, "I assure you that I shall regret it for you if fate have denied you a better choice. But at all events" (constrainedly), "I must thank you for the gracious and successful manner in which you have kept suspicion from becoming certainty before time proves it so."

She looked fully at him this time, and smiled.

"Gratitude comes hard to you," she said. "There is no cause for it in anything I have ever done. You may be sure it was not to please you at all, but to gratify something in myself that demanded satisfaction. Now, please explain to me what you mean by your extraordinary summary of things we know too well, and how I have offended you when I am really your friend—yours, and "— She stopped, a smile flitted over her face and was gone; it revealed for the unnamed person a gentleness and an affection that perhaps she did not care to have her tones betray.

"Yes, you have offended me," he said. "I have no right to comment on your actions in general."

"None whatever."

"But what I do have a right to demand is an explanation from you of conduct so strange as to be unaccountable."

She flushed a little.

" It's not pleasant," she answered, " when one has done the best that opened up to be told that it's unaccountable conduct."

" Then it was you? I was sure of it." She looked at him earnestly.

" Why should there be any beating about the bush?" she answered. " I should like it better if you need never have known ; but, since you were sure to find it out sooner or later, it might as well come now. What I have done is wise and right, the most satisfactory thing to me, and to others wiser than I. But I wish you would never speak of it."

" Never speak of your coming forward with your whole fortune to make up the loss that this fellow's claim will be to us? Never speak of it ! " cried Archdale. " And accept it? From you? You certainly have a flattering opinion of me."

" If it were like any business losses," she said, " it would be different. But this is something nobody could have been prepared for ; it needs something outside of the routine to meet it." She waited a moment. " Will you put your case, as you said you were going to do?" she asked. " It will make it clearer, and you will see that there is nothing extraordinary. I think you need not say anything more about — about us, that is all understood. Go on from there."

" A father and a son, then, are nominally in business together," he answered ; " the father does the work ; the son has a generous share of the profits. Matters are going on swimmingly. Suddenly a claimant turns up who wants a grand slice of the property. He is the only son of the father's elder brother, — a being who was not known to have existed, that is, who was supposed to have died when an infant. The father, my father, was named for him, and my grandfather's will gave the largest share of his fortune to his oldest son, Walter, whom he supposed to be my father, but who was really Gerald Edmonson's father — if the fellow's proofs turn out valid ; they are having a thorough overhauling. My uncle does not suffer ; it is only we. I am sorry," he added, " that you are liable to be in any way connected with loss, but at the worst it is so remotely that it will never affect you. As for the other matter, the story," — he stopped with a movement of irritation, perhaps of some deeper feeling, — " that must be borne as best it can, nothing of that falls upon you, certainly. How the matter concerns a young lady at all I can't imagine ; so I fail to see what interest you can have in it, or what right to move in it."

" You fail to see?" she said and gave him a smile full of sweetness. It was not a coaxing smile, as if she begged him to reconsider his opinions ; it indorsed her own while placidly acquiescing in mutual indifference. "Besides, do you know it was through me that the portrait was found?" And she gave him an account of the discovery. He did not think it necessary to interrupt her by saying that he had heard Edmonson give it with great relish ; it seemed a good opportunity to learn whether he had been telling the truth. The story was substantially the same, but the enjoyment of the narrator was absent. " And, then," she added, finishing, " this is not a bad investment."

"It may be now; I can't tell. We were under full sail; we have large ventures, and to give out so much ready money may mean ruin. In a few months, perhaps sooner, you may have the happiness of bearing a bankrupt name."

Elizabeth's eyes were full of pity at the bitter tones in which she heard suffering; she looked away and answered: —

"It is merely justice to me to let me prevent that, if I can."

"Good heavens!" he cried; and, struck with the readiness of her answer, he studied her face. He would have liked to be sure from what motive she was acting. Was it pride, or really pity? The thought of the last made him furious; the other was at least endurable. "And you might not prevent it," he added, watching to catch her eyes as she should turn them back to answer. He was reasonably sure that it was pride.

"Then let me do this for my own sake," she said. "Listen to me calmly for a moment. There is one thing you ought not to forget. Either I am your wife, which God forbid, and I believe he has forbidden it, or I am simply Katie's friend. In case of the first, — if I have destroyed your happiness and Katie's, and my own, — what can money do for me? Life offers me nothing; there are no possibilities before me so far as joy is concerned; there is nothing left for me but to do the best I know how; we must pick up the little things that lie along the way in life, you and I; there will be nothing else for us; I have made you suffer so much, and you deny me this little thing that can never balance any pain, but is all I can do? Why are you so unwise? Why should we make ourselves more miserable than we need be?"

He sprang up. These very words — that he had often said to himself in regard to his own life, that in effect he had said to her that morning — how harsh they were, how they cut him! He was tender with his wounded vanity. What man would like to hear that a woman has nothing before her but misery if she be bound to himself?

"There is one condition," he cried, harshly, "under which I will accept your money, — when you love me; when it is the gift of love." He laughed bitterly. "I am safe," he said.

"Yes, Mr. Archdale, you are safe," she answered, rising to meet him as he stood before her. "I can use no such weapons. It is beneath you to do it. To say such a thing to me when you know that in any event my great blessing is that I don't care a pin's worth for you, that I am not a sighing woman wasting her affection on you, while you — But I don't suppose you meant your words as an insult."

"Have I ever been rude to you?" he asked, eagerly. "Such a thing would be an infinite disgrace to me."

"Yes," she said, answering his assertion.

"'While you,'" he repeated, "you said 'while you' — What were you going to say about me?"

"While you love Katie with all your heart," she answered, "as it is right you should do." He looked at her, and remembered that for all her courage it might be that he owed her at least the courtesy of all observances of respect and regard before others. He had committed an unpardonable error that day of the dinner at his father's, and he felt a confusion, as if the color were coming to his face now as he thought of it.

" You — mistake," he stammered. " I assure you you do. I think I understand — I " —

She looked up at him. Her face was pale, and there was in it the kind of compassion that one might imagine a spirit to feel for a way-worn mortal.

" You owe me no explanation," she said. ' Let us believe in the victory of the right, and put this nightmare away from us. Remember you are speaking only to Katie's friend."

He looked at her, and he could not be sure.

" But you must let me speak," he said, " because I see you mistake. I don't want you to think because — I confess it — her beauty has a great fascination for me that I can forget myself, that I — it was like admiring a beautiful living picture."

She moved nearer, involuntarily.

" Poor fellow ! " she said under her breath, " you have been brave ; you are brave, very brave. I've seen it." Then, after a pause in which she retreated a little and stood considering deeply, she said, " I will tell you something ; it would be too much to be spoken of, only that you don't understand why I did this thing about the business. Think how I am placed. I may be standing between my dear friend and the man who was to have been her husband, and separating them forever. That night when I came home from your father's I realized it more than ever before ; it filled me so that I could not bear the thought of life. I happened to have something by me, and I — almost took it. I should have slipped away from between you two, I was so bent upon doing it, —only, the warning saved me from such a sin. It will never be again," she added as she saw his eyes dilate with questioning horror. " That temptation has gone. I have accepted my lot, for it was permitted to come, or even that wicked man could not have brought it. But now, think, think how I must long to do some little thing, not to atone, that's impossible, but to make life not quite so hard to you, and to her. Now, this has come for you. Take it, I entreat you. Some day I may be able to help her in some way ; I think it will be so."

He looked into her eyes as she raised them to his.

" But you didn't mean to — do all this, if it is done," he said. " There's no need of talking about atoning, as if you were guilty of anything."

" But, then, I ought to have refused ; it was my place. It would have saved everything."

" You wanted to," he said, " and you yielded to oblige Katie."

She looked relieved at his answer. It surprised him ; he wondered that he had remembered her hesitation.

"You will do this thing?" she persisted. "You see it is your duty."

"Do you know the reason you are so anxious to have me do it?" he asked, the momentary softening of his face gone. "It's out of no love for Katie, or friendliness to me."

"No," she said to his last statement, and added, "Yes, I know; I've seen it."

"What is it?"

"I suppose," she said, humbly, "that it's my pride.

"Yes," he cried, "that's what it is — your pride. Well, I have my pride, too. I'll take your money, when you love me — when it's the gift of your love, as I said — no sooner; I shall have to do without it this year, I'm afraid."

Her eyes swept him from head to foot in an indignant glance. Then she turned and walked away as if disdaining further speech. He bowed in silence as he opened the door for her, looking at her with a mocking smile, and even as he did so taking in every line of her graceful figure, the pose of her head, and the flush upon her face. In answer to the taunt she did speak one sentence under her breath, but he caught it: —

"You are not the only one," she said.

When he had closed the door after her he walked slowly the length of the room, and, standing by the window, in another moment saw her pass by on her way to the shore where she had learned that the party had gone. If they were already sailing it was no matter; she could wait for them there, or come back; but they might not have started, and to put any part of sea and land between herself and Archdale would be a joy to her.

Archdale watched her until she disappeared.

"And I called myself proud," he muttered. He stood lost in revery, living the scene over again. "What eyes!" he thought; "they're as unconscious as a child's, but such power as they have; they call out a man's best, and I met her with my worst. I never even told her she was generous. She meant to be kind when she humiliated me so." And then he thought that she deserved a better fate than to be bound to him whose heart was with Katie, and realized that Elizabeth was not at all the kind of woman whom he should choose to set his love upon. Yet he smiled scornfully at himself for the eager start with which he had cried out that if she were roused she could be magnificent. A magnificent woman was not in his line, and if it proved that she was his wife, she would go through the world a sleeping princess, he said to himself, unless he should go off to the wars and get shot. Perhaps that would be the best way out of the difficulty, he thought, and would leave her free. At the moment Edmonson's face rose before him, and he frowned as he wondered what feeling there was in that quarter. "No, no," he said to himself. "Not Edmonson. I know he's a villain; I feel it." He interrupted his thoughts by asking, sarcastically, what it could all matter to himself, well out of harm's way, what happened, what Elizabeth or anybody else did? He was very angry with her, and she did not realize the Archdale unforgiveness. If she had, would she have cared? She had not yielded her purpose.

CHAPTER XXI.

WAR CLOUDS.

"I HATE November," cried Mrs. Eveleigh, coming into Elizabeth's room and bringing a whiff of cold air with her. "It's a mean month," she continued. "There's nothing but disagreeable things about it. The leaves are all gone, and the snow hasn't come. You can't even go out riding with any comfort, the ground is so frozen you are jolted to pieces." And with step emphasizing the petulance of her voice, the speaker turned from her companion and went to her own room, to put away her bonnet and the heavy cloak that, if it had not been able to protect her from the roughness of the roads, had kept the cold air from doing more than biting revengefully at her nose and the tips of her fingers, in place of all the mischief it would have been glad to inflict if it had had the chance. The steps grown fainter, went about the next room, and Elizabeth went on with her reading only half attentively, watching for the inevitable coming back. "But then," resumed Mrs. Eveleigh, returning to her subject as soon as she had opened the door wide enough to admit her voice, "one must see a little of the world sometimes. I'm coming in to warm my feet by your fire, shan't I? mine is low. I declare, it's hard that Nancy should be so partial to you. I can get scarcely any attention, though, to be sure, poor thing, it's well to have it from somebody, even if it is from dependents. And you don't get any too much from the quarter where you've a right to it."

Elizabeth, knowing it would be useless to attempt going on with her reading, had laid aside her book on Mrs. Eveleigh's entrance, and now she looked up from the sewing toward which she had reached out her hand, and said ; —

. "You know as well as I do that it is exactly as I want it. Mr. Archdale considers my wishes, and as to having a right, you know, Cousin Patience, that that is what is being disproved now. Haven't I declared that the ceremony was nothing at all?"

"Oh, certainly you have, but you'll find out how little good that will do. I have not an idea that you'll ever have a chance to say ' Yes ' to that splendid Edmonson. You'll find it out soon enough, poor child."

Elizabeth flushed, then turned pale.

"Have you heard anything?" she asked.

"Not yet ; not since that Mr. Harwin turned out a minister, just as I thought he would, and your case went to the court to be decided. You'll have the first news, I suppose, but I don't doubt what it will be."

"Neither do I," returned the girl, resolutely.

"We shall see," said Mrs. Eveleigh. "Do you know," she added, "that Mr. Edmonson came yesterday when you were out?"

"Yes."

Then there fell between the pair as long an interval of silence as Mrs. Eveleigh ever permitted where she was concerned. She broke it by asking, energetically : —

"Elizabeth, if you really believed that you were not Mr. Archdale's wife, why, in the name of wonder, did you go and put your whole fortune into his business? And why did your father let you?"

"My father had no legal right to interfere," said the girl, ignoring the first question, "and he did not choose to strain his authority. When was he ever unkind to me?"

"I think he was then, decidedly." And the speaker nodded her head with emphasis. "But you have not told me why you did it," she continued.

Elizabeth was silent a moment. "I had been the means of the whole thing being discovered," she said, "and I had hurt him enough already."

"And he let you risk your whole fortune just because you had happened to put your finger through a hole in the hall tapestry."

"No," cried Elizabeth, "he did no such thing. He is very angry with me now because I invested it; he is not willing, even though he knows that it's for Katie's sake."

"I thought you said just now that it was for Mr. Archdale's." Elizabeth looked at her, and smiled triumphantly.

"I did," she answered. "It's the same thing; I have always told you so."

"Um!" said Mrs. Eveleigh, and returned to the attack. "If he wouldn't take the money, how could you give it?" The girl was silent. "It was the father, I know ; they say a penny never comes amiss to him."

"How did you find this out, Cousin Patience?" But Mrs. Eveleigh laughed instead of answering. "You have not spoken of it?" cried Elizabeth.

"Not a word. Why, I don't want to proclaim any one of, my own family a goose." The only answer was a smile of satisfaction. "You don't mind being called a goose, I see," pursued the speaker.

"Not at all. I know it's often true. Only it doesn't happen to be true here."

Though Mrs. Eveleigh had so openly criticised Elizabeth, it would have gone ill with any one who had dared to follow her example. She was often annoyed by things in Elizabeth ; but she believed in the girl's truth more than she did in her own. And there she was quite right. Now she began to talk about the portrait scene, and declared that Mr. Edmonson looked very handsome standing beside the old picture that he so much resembled.

"That portrait was Colonel Archdale's grandfather, his mother's

father, Mr. Edmonson," explained Elizabeth, perceiving that her companion's ideas were somewhat mixed. And then Mrs. Eveleigh confessed
that she had been trying to explain about the portrait and the relation-
ship, and that though she had talked learnedly about the matter, she had
been a little confused in her own mind.

"This portrait was in the colonel's father's house, lent him to be copied,
and when he fled he took the original with him, and left the copy. It
was a duel that he fought, and there was something irregular that he did
about it. He went to Virginia, you remember, and while there he
changed his name. Then he came here, and the search for him died
out. The matter was hushed up some way, I suppose."

"And pretended that he belonged to a different race of Archdales in
another part of England," asserted Mrs. Eveleigh, contemptuously.

"Perhaps we should, too, if we had been in his place."

"What! in his place, Elizabeth? Can you even imagine how you
would feel if you had murdered anybody, or about the same as that?"

"Yes."

"Nonsense, my dear. You must have a powerful imagination; I
shouldn't think it was healthy. There's no use, any way, in being so odd."

"No."

"First 'yes,' and then 'no,' and neither of them means anything.
But if you haven't anything to say, I wish you would tell me how those
people, the colonel's father and mother, happened to have a son living
that they didn't know anything about."

Elizabeth, full of remembrance of the time when a human life, even if
her own, had seemed light to her, could not help smiling at Mrs. Eveleigh's literal interpretation of things. "They had to escape at once," she
said, "and the doctor said the child would die if he undertook a sea-
voyage in that state. So she sent him to her father's home with a
nurse who was very fond of him; he was a baby then. And she went
away with her husband with the understanding that when the child re-
covered, as the doctor expected him to do, the nurse should bring him to
her in America. And she left open some way of communication. But,
instead of the baby, there came news that he was dead."

"And he wasn't dead?"

"No; his grandfather adopted him, and gave him his name. He hated
Mr. Archdale; he had lost his daughter through him, and he determined
to keep the child. So he bribed the nurse to report his death, and per-
suaded her that it was better for the little fellow to stay with him as his
sole heir than follow the fortunes of a haunted man in a wilderness, as
America must have been then."

"And do you really believe they never knew of this son of theirs being
alive?"

"Mr. Archdale's will, if nothing else, proves that. He had three
sons here, you remember; and the colonel, the eldest of these, was
named Walter, after the one supposed to have died in England. And,

now, you see how this trouble all happened. The will left the greater part of the property to Mr. Archdale's oldest son, Walter, whom he supposed the colonel. But the real oldest son, Walter, was this Mr. Edmonson's father. So that the colonel was really left penniless."

"Yes, yes, now I see," cried Mrs. Eveleigh. "You are like your father when you come to explanations, Elizabeth; a person can always get at what you mean. Now tell me about the portrait, how it came there, and how in the world Mr. Edmonson found it."

"I don't know how it came there," she answered, leading away from the rest of the question by adding, "I have never asked a word about it."

"Elizabeth! you *are* odd, that's certain. And if Mr. Archdale is never coming here any more, you will never have a chance now to ask him. It's a pity to be so diffident."

Elizabeth smiled a little. "What else did you hear this morning?" she asked.

"Nothing that will interest you, though of course I thought it would when I heard it. Stephen Archdale has come back from his expedition up to the Penobscots with Colonel Pepperell. I wonder how they succeeded?"

"I can tell you that. The Indians have sent word that they will not fight against their brothers of St. John's and New Brunswick. That means that they'll fight for them. We shall have an Indian war with the French one. Think of the horrors of it." She shuddered as she spoke.

"Yes," returned Mrs. Eveleigh, with calm acquiescence. "It will be dreadful for the people that live in the little villages and in the open country."

This calmness, as if one were gazing from an impregnable fortress upon the tortures and deaths of others, silenced Elizabeth. She looked the speaker over slowly and turned away.

"Any more news?" asked Mrs. Eveleigh in a cheerful tone.

"I can tell you nothing more," returned Elizabeth.

This was literally true. It would not have been true if she had said that she had heard nothing else, for she had been sitting with her father for an hour, and had learned of a secret scheme, — a scheme so daring that the very idea of it made her eyes kindle and her breath come quickly,— a scheme that if it should fail would be hooted at as the dream of vainglorious madmen, and if it should succeed, would be called a stroke of genius — magnificent. It interested her to know that among the most eager to carry out the scheme was Major Vaughn, the man whose valor she had asserted to Sir Temple Dacre a few months before. A small band of men had pledged themselves to put reality into this dream of grand achievement. "Its failure means," thought Elizabeth, "that America is to be French and Jesuit; its success that Englishmen, and liberty of mind and conscience, rule here." She prayed and hoped for success, and took an eager interest in all the details of the scheme that had reached her; but these were meagre enough, for, as yet, it was only outlined; the main thing was that it was resolved upon. The prisoners captured at Canso had been at last exchanged. They had been brought to Boston, and had given valuable information about the place of their captivity, the stronghold of France in America. Governor Shirley had declared that Louisburg was to be captured, and that Colonel Pepperell was the man to do it. Elizabeth, as she looked across at Mrs. Eveleigh, wondered what she would say to the project. But she wondered in silence, not only because silence had been enjoined, but because this was not a woman to trust with the making of great events. She had heard of an Indian war, and her chief thought had been that she would be safe.

The war had been talked about all the autumn. It was a terrible necessity, but this new direction that it was to take was something worth pondering over.

Elizabeth naturally, took large views of things, and, as her father's companion, she had not learned to restrict them. But, also, for the last months she had perceived dimly that there was a power within her which might never be called into action. And this power rose, sometimes, with vehemence against the monotony of her surroundings, in the midst of her wealth of comforts and of affection.

It was the last of November, only two days after this conversation, that Stephen Archdale was announced.

"He has come to tell me the decision," said Elizabeth to Mrs. Eveleigh; "he promised he would come immediately. It's good news."

"Then what makes you so pale? And you're actually trembling."

Elizabeth looked at her companion in surprise, for all her years of acquaintance with her.

"Don't you understand?" she said. "The strain is to be taken off. The certainty must be good; and yet there is the possibility that it is not. This and the thought that the moment has come make me tremble."

As she was speaking she moved away and in another moment was in the drawing-room with Archdale.

"You have brought me word," she said, as soon as her greeting was over. "You have good news; I see it in your eyes."

"Yes," he answered. "I suppose you will call it good news. You are free; you are still Mistress Royal."

She clasped her hands impulsively, and retreated a few steps. It seemed to him as he watched her that her first emotion was a thankfulness as deep as a prayer. He saw that she could not speak. Then she came up to him holding out both her hands.

"Never was any one so welcome to me as you with your words this morning," she said. "I have not spoiled your life and Katie's."

"And you are free," he said again.

"Yes," she repeated, "I am free." And as she drew away her hands she made a movement almost imperceptible and instantly checked, as if she had thrown off some heavy weight. He read it, however, as he stood there with his eyes upon her face, which was bright with a thankfulness and a beauty that, although he had seen something of her possibilities of expression, he had never dreamed of. How glad she was! A pang went through him. He understood it afterward. It had meant that he was asking himself if Katie's face, when he told her the news, would look so happy at having gained him as this girl did at having lost him; and he had not been sure of it. All the autumn there had been strange fancies in his head about Katie. He had had no right, under the circumstances, to send Lord Bulchester away; but it had seemed strange to him that any girl's love of power should be carried so far if it were mere love of power that moved her. But no shadow on Elizabeth's face showed him that she dreamed of change in Katie, and Stephen felt rebuked that friendship could find its object more perfect than love did.

"Will the wedding be on the anniversary of the other one?" asked Elizabeth. "I suppose it will," she added; "Katie ought to have it so. That will come in three weeks. It will be a little time before you sail, if you go." And she smiled rather sadly, then glanced about her to make sure that the last remark had not been overheard.

"Ah!" he said, "I see you know all about the scheme on foot. But it is safe to trust you. You are very much interested," he added, watching her.

"Very much. My father does trust me a good deal. But I hope I shall not make him sorry for it."

Archdale kept on looking at her, and smiling.

"You prefer making people glad," he answered.

"But perhaps you will not go — now?" she said.

"Oh, yes. I promised my services to Colonel Pepperell last summer; that holds me, you see. Besides, I want to do my part."

"I could not imagine you standing idle by while others were striking the blows for our country," said Elizabeth. "Katie has told me a good deal about you at one time and another. Dear Katie!" she added in an undertone, with an exquisite gentleness in her face. Then, looking back from the window where her eyes had wandered, she turned off her emotion by some gay speech.

Very soon afterward the young man left her. For he was on his way to carry the news to Katie who was then in Boston visiting her aunt. But to go to her he passed Mr. Royal's door, and his wishes, as well as his promise, made him delay his own happiness for a moment to see Elizabeth rejoice. He saw her rejoice to his heart's content; and then he took leave of her for his happy meeting with his betrothed.

[TO BE CONTINUED.]

EDITOR'S TABLE.

EVIDENCES are constantly multiplying that American history is a subject which has not lost its interest to investigators or to readers. During the past month four distinct works, namely, the fifth volume of Von Holst's Constitutional History of the United States, the third of Schouler's History of the United States, the second of McMaster's History of the People of the United States, and also a new volume of Hubert Howe Bancroft's History of the Pacific States, have been published, and are destined, no doubt, to take their places as "standards." This diligence on the part of their respective writers, and the interest in them manifested by the great public is commendable, and in a measure dispels the oft-repeated saying that Americans are a nation of novel-readers.

It is gratifying, also, to record another fact. During the third week in July the Old South lectures for young people, illustrative of "The War for the Union," were inaugurated in Boston. The ancient "meeting-house" was crowded with earnest students to hear the first lecture on slavery, delivered, by William Lloyd Garrison, Jr. The speaker gave a vivid sketch of the chief events of the anti-slavery movement, and of the part taken by George Thompson, Garrison, Phillips, Whittier, and Harriet Martineau.

***

Students of the anti-slavery struggle should not forget, however, how much the success of that struggle was due to Mrs. Maria Weston Chapman, whose death occurred at Weymouth, Mass., on July 12. She was not only a *magna pars* of the struggle, but one of the most remarkable women of our time. Mrs. Maria Child used to relate how Mrs. Chapman, clad in the height of fashion of that day, came into the first anti-slavery fair, an entire stranger to every one present. "She looked around over the few tables, scantily supplied, and stopped by some faded artificial flowers. The poor commodity only indicated the utter poverty of means to carry on the work. We thought her a spy, or maybe she was a slave-holder." From that time she entered heartily into the work. She became the life of the Female Anti-slavery Society in Boston, she spoke often in public; her pen was never idle when it could advance the cause of equal rights and freedom.

Mr. Lowell, in his rhymed letter, descriptive of an anti-slavery bazaar at Faneuil Hall, and the celebrities of the cause there assembled, drew the portrait of this gifted woman with his usual felicitous touch: —

> " There was Maria Chapman, too,
> With her swift eyes of clear steel-blue,
> The coiled up mainspring of the Fair,
> Originating everywhere
> The expansive force, without a sound,
> That whirls a hundred wheels around;
> Herself meanwhile as calm and still
> As the bare crown of Prospect Hill;
> A noble woman, brave and apt,
> Cumæa's sybil not more rapt,
> Who might, with those fair tresses shorn,
> The Maid of Orleans' casque have worn;
> Herself the Joan of our Arc,
> For every shaft a shining mark."

***

IT is one thing to be a good ship-builder for the government, and quite another thing to be in favor with the Secretary of the Navy, at Washington. This is the lesson, and the only lesson, which can be deduced from the two dispatches which have been transmitted over the country, namely: that the "Dolphin" has been rejected, and that John Roach, her builder, has failed.

The case has its value as a warning to American ship-builders. They are given to understand that the closest compliance with the requisitions of the department in the process of constructing a vessel, and that under the direction of experts, perfectly competent to determine what is good work and what is bad, will avail them nothing unless they are in favor with the Secretary when the vessel is offered for acceptance. And they are warned that the Department of Justice holds it perfectly legal for the Navy Department to lay upon them such conditions as to construction as must determine the capacity of the vessel for speed, and yet reject the vessel as not fast enough. They may be fined heavily for not having used their discretion, and yet may have been denied discretion as to the plans used.

It will be remembered by all who have watched the case, that the "Dolphin" was found satisfactory and in full accordance with the terms of the contract by one naval board, and that it was then condemned by another board of no greater weight or capacity. If this fact be remembered, it should be weighed with the full understanding that naval officers, chosen by Mr. Whitney for this service, are just as much dependents of the new Secretary as their predecessors were of Mr. Chandler. The last set of officials, as experts, were not superior to those which constituted the first; and yet Mr. Whitney bases his refusal to accept the vessel upon the contradiction of the first report to the second. If the first report was worthless, why not the second, in the light of all the facts?

What is needed to-day is a board of examiners fully competent to pronounce on the merits, of not only the "Dolphin" but of any and every other ship that shall be built, and fully sundered from, and independent of, political and official relations with the Navy Department. The nearest approach to this is the report of the body of experts — ship-builders, and ship-captains, experts in ship's materials, and the like — whom Mr. Roach invited to examine the "Dolphin." The report of these gentlemen flatly contradicts Mr. Whitney's board on points which are matters of fact, and not of opinion, and therefore throws the burden of proof upon Mr. Whitney himself. Until some equally unpolitical and unofficial body refutes it, the treatment Mr. Roach has received will be set down to other motives than the best.

₊

THE republic at last bows its head in sorrow at the death of its greatest citizen. In awe and admiration it honors the character which, heroic to the last, has never been more conspicuously shown than during the months of that depressing illness, the end of which must have been to him a welcome entering into rest.

The same unquailing courage, and the same calm, grim fortitude which shed their fadeless lustre upon his whole extraordinary career were evinced by General Grant at the last moments of his life. For months the nation has hung over his bedside, awaiting the silent foot-fall of the unseen conqueror of all that is mortal.

The nation's loss is not measured by the vacant place. For nearly a decade General Grant had been only a private citizen, wielding no sceptre of authority, and exercising no sway in the public councils. And yet his going is a loss; for he was everywhere felt, not merely by what he had done, but by what he was, — one of the great reserve forces of our national commonwealth.

"Great men," said Burke, "are the guideposts and landmarks of the State." General Grant was the guidepost of a victorious war, and a landmark of a magnanimous peace. A pillar of strength has fallen; and yet a broken shaft is not the fit emblem of his life. It is a finished and splendid column, crowned with its full glory.

The chieftain is dead. The American people themselves will now judge him, after the calm evening and the serene repose of retirement, more justly than in the stress and storm of struggle. The asperities of angry contentions have passed; the flaws have faded, and the blemishes are dimmed, while the splendor of General Grant's achievements and the simple grandeur of his character have gained a brighter halo as the years have rolled by. The clouds and the smoke of battle have long since lifted; the fragments and the scenes are swallowed in the majestic drama; and to-day we see the hero elevated on his true pedestal of fame through the just perspective of history.

It is given to few men to bear suffering with the fortitude displayed by the departed hero; it is given to fewer still to await in patience and without complaint the certain issue of suffering in death. But it is neither his fortitude, nor his patience, nor his touching solicitude, nor his unselfish industry which distinguished him in an almost unique degree. It was rather, in one word, his simplicity, his strong but unpretentious character, and his firm but magnanimous nature.

Of such, plainly, is the kingdom of Heaven, and it is a national glory that of such, too, in the instance of General Grant, the American people was never neglectful.

IF every person who is inclined to attribute to Socialism all the discontent now prevalent among the laboring classes of this country, would carefully read Mr. Laurence Gronlund's remarkable book, entitled, *The Coöperative Commonwealth*, — an exposition of modern Socialism, — he would perhaps awaken to a comprehension of the fact that true Socialism is neither communism, nor lawlessness, nor anarchy. We wish this book could be scattered, by millions, among the intelligent people of this land, if for no other purpose than to root out many of the false ideas which are current, as well as to inculcate a logical explanation of much that is transpiring at the present moment.

We are told that at least 30,000 laborers are out of work in Cincinnati, and that full as many are unemployed in Chicago. The same state of affairs prevails in other large cities. These people, we are also told by the newspapers, are " exposed to the designs of socialistic leaders, and liable to embrace their dangerous schemes." Hence, it is to be inferred, of course, that timely measures should be instituted to " guard the unreflecting against socialistic theories and measures."

Despair sometimes calls for a desperate remedy. When men are in physical or financial distress they *are* apt to lose their heads, so to speak, and to be subject to the wildest delusions and hallucinations. A great many of the unfortunates now out

of employment have been already reduced to misery and want; but it is a mistake to suppose that the philosophy of Socialism can afford them any relief or consolation, or that it can incite them to mad deeds of violence. There are certain demagogues in this country who, assuming to be Socialists, are ready to stir up the popular mind, even to the shedding of blood; but such men are few in numbers, and wield only a limited influence.

Now, Socialism holds that the impending reconstruction of society, which Huxley predicts, will be brought about by the logic of events, and teaches that the coming revolution, which every intelligent mind must foresee, is strictly an evolution. Socialists of this school reason from no assumed first principle, like the French, who start from " social equality," or like Herbert Spencer, who lays it down as an axiom that " every man has freedom to do all that he wills, provided he infringes not the like freedom of every other man;" but basing themselves squarely on *experience*, — not individual but universal experience, — they can, and do present clear-cut, definite solutions.

It is this true *German* Socialism which Mr. Gronlund, in the work previously alluded to, very clearly presents, and which should be more generally understood than it is.

Apropos of the subject, it will not be amiss to recall a statement made by Frederic Harrison, namely : —

" The working-class is the only class which is not a class. It is the nation. It represents, so to speak, the body as a whole, of which the other classes only represent special organs. These organs, no doubt, have great and indispensable functions, but for most purposes of government the state consists of the vast laboring majority. Its welfare depends on what their lives are like."

And this from Carlyle : —

" It is not to die, or even to die of hunger that makes a man wretched : many men have died; all men must die. But it is to live miserable, we know not why; to work sore and yet gain nothing; to be heartworn, weary, yet isolated, unrelated, girt in with a cold universal *Laissez-faire*."

AMONG THE BOOKS.

It seems but a short time since we pored interestedly over the pages of Mr. Stanley's "Through the Dark Continent," which described the exploration of the Congo in 1876-7, from Nyongwe to the Atlantic Ocean. The final results of that first expedition, which surpasses all anticipation, are now recorded in two handsome volumes from the same pen, bearing the title: *The Congo and the Founding of Its Free State*.[1] When Mr. Stanley, in 1878, had crossed the African continent and had reached the mouth of the Congo, he took ship for Europe. He had reached Marseilles, where, in the railway-station, he was met by two commissioners who had been sent by Leopold II., King of the Belgians, for the express purpose of interesting Mr. Stanley in the' project entertained by that king of founding a State in the heart of Africa. This project was subsequently accepted, and all the powers of Europe entered into the scheme. Mr. Stanley now relates, for the first time, the story of the founding, — a story which is as entertaining as the liveliest piece of fiction, and as marvellous in its unfolding as would be the sudden discovery of a new and habitable world. From the mouth of the Congo to Stanley Falls is about fifteen hundred miles, and the basin of this immense river contains more than a million and a half square miles; that is, a territory nearly one-half as large as that of the United States. The opening of this great country to the commerce of the world is one of the greatest events of the nineteenth, indeed of any, century. By the agreement of the sovereigns of Europe, no European power is ever to be permitted to seize the sea-coasts of the continent, or to levy differential customs and high tariffs upon the commerce of the world such as our New England and Middle States now levy upon the West and South. Forever hereafter a merchant or producer dwelling in the Congo can dispose of his ivory and ebony, or any other product whatsoever, in whatever market it will yield him the most money, and buy his shovel and hoe, his gunpowder, and the like, where he can buy them the best and the cheapest. It is, perhaps, not too much to affirm that the founding of such an empire on such a basis will make in time as great a change in commercial affairs as the establishment of the American Republic has made in political affairs and in the relation of men to governments. The work of Mr. Stanley is destined to have a large influence. It is the most important book on Africa that has ever been written at any period of time or in any language. And yet no record of good deeds grandly done could savor of more modesty and unpretentiousness than does the narrative in these two noble volumes.

———

Miss Anna Laurens Dawes, the daughter of Senator Dawes, of Massachusetts, has undertaken "an explanation of the Constitution and government of the United States," in her book entitled *How We are Governed*.[2] Believing, as we do, that a knowledge of politics is an essential part of education, we hail this work as one of the hopeful signs of the times, and commend it especially to young people, because the author has so accurately and comprehensively accomplished her task as to make it worthy of confidence. Simplicity in writing is the first needed qualification of one who undertakes to instruct youth. Miss Dawes exhibits this quality, and takes nothing for granted as to the previous knowledge of her readers. Her plan follows the order of the Constitution, and that document is quoted in full, and in its several parts under the division of "The Legislature," "The Executive," "The Citizen," and "The States."

[1] The Congo and the Founding of Its Free State. By Henry M. Stanley. 2 vols. Maps and Illustrations. New York: Harper & Bros. Price, $10.00.

[2] How We are Governed. By Anna Laurens Dawes. Boston: D. Lothrop & Co.

It is the practical nature of the contents of *The Hunter's Handbook*[1] which will commend it to all readers, and which stamps it as an indispensable work for all persons who "go camping out." This is just the season for such healthful recreation and resting among the hills or along shore. It is just the season, too, when, unless he knows exactly how to manage, the camper-out is subjected to a great many annoyances as well as pleasures. The little work under notice contains many valuable hints and suggestions, while its notes of all camp requisites and receipts are exceedingly valuable. Some of the author's quaint aphorisms on camp economy, camp neatness and cleanliness, and on the signs and portents of the weather, will tend to keep the reader in good humor. It would require years of experience for new beginners to acquire the information which a half hour's study of this book will easily impart. To all such, then, it is invaluable.

THE first volume of Mr. McMaster's entertaining work on the *History of the People of the United States*[2] appeared just three years ago this summer, and the lively interest which it then aroused gave promise of the cordial welcome that would be generally extended to future volumes of the same work. The first volume closed with the year 1790. The second volume, which has recently been published, continues the easy and entertaining narrative down to 1803. Within its seven chapters there is a vast fund of valuable information in regard to life and society as they existed under the early administrations. These chapters cover the experimental years of the Republic under the Constitution, — the years which, so susceptible of popular treatment, are so particularly engaging to students of American history. At so formative a period in the

national development, when there was open contest between Congress and the States, when the group of undoubted aristocrats gathered around Hamilton were in direct opposition to the extreme republicanism of the circle which acknowledged Jefferson as its chief, the dominance of English or French influence was an element of great moment to the future of the nation. Mr. McMaster has most admirably handled this phase of his subject.

The account of town and country life as they were at the beginning of the present century, and of the growth of those social usages which we have come almost to regard as instinctive, is very entertaining and instructive. Barring certain blemishes and a few inaccuracies, which ought to be excusable in a work of such character, Mr. McMaster's two volumes form a very valuable and welcome contribution to our national literature. It was a felicitous thought which prompted him to enter this peculiar field, and to gather up the important facts which writers on political history have generally avoided. So thoroughly and so admirably has Mr. McMaster worked this field that we doubt whether any other writer, coming after him, will be tempted to invade the same territory. The work thus far ends with the negotiations which led to the Louisiana purchase, and we are led to expect three more instalments before it shall be completed.

SHOULD any readers be tempted by Mrs. Gould's article in this number of THE BAY STATE MONTHLY to visit Nantucket, they will do well to take with them, for handy reference and trustworthy guidance, Mr. Godfrey's *Island of Nantucket: What it was and what it is.*[3] It is a complete index and guide to all that is interesting in the island, — tells just how to get there and what to see there, — and contains, moreover, several special articles, by different hands, on the history, botany, geology, and entomology of the island. The maps accompanying the text were made expressly for the book.

[1] The Hunter's Handbook, containing a description of all articles required in camp, with hints on provisions and stores, and receipts for camp cooking. By "An Old Hunter." Boston: Lee & Shepard. Price, 50 cents.

[2] A History of the People of the United States, from the Revolution to the Civil War. By John Bach McMaster. Vol. II. New York: D. Appleton & Co. Price, $2.50.

[3] The Island of Nantucket: What it was and what it is. Compiled by Edward K. Godfrey. Boston: Lee & Shepard. Price, paper, 50 cents.

A FITTING companion to Mr. Wallace's "Malay Archipelago," which appeared some ten or a dozen years ago, is a new book. entitled *A Naturalist's Wanderings in the Eastern Archipelago*,[1] of which Henry O. Forbes is the author. Mr. Forbes revisited most of the islands which Mr. Wallace had described, but his route in each island was altogether different. He gives us the first detailed account of the Timor-laut Islands, with very interesting and valuable ethnological notes. The work is divided into six parts, devoted to the Cocos-Keeling Islands, Java, Sumatra, the Moluccas, Timor-laut, Buru, and Timor. Many illustrations are interspersed throughout the text, and the whole work is exceedingly vigorous, graphic, and abounding in interest.

Under the Rays of the Aurora Borealis; In the Land of the Lapps and Kvæns,[2] by Sophus Tromholt, edited by Carl Siewers, furnishes a narrative of journeys in Lapland, Finland, and Northern Russia in 1882–83. It also contains an account of the recent circumpolar scientific expedi-

[1] Wanderings of a Naturalist in the Eastern Archipelago. By H. O. Forbes. Illustrated. New York: Harper & Bros. Price, $5.00.

[2] Under the Rays of the Aurora Borealis; In the Land of the Lapps and Kvæns. By Sophus Tromholt. Boston: Houghton, Mifflin, & Co.

tions, and a popular statement of what is known of the Aurora Borealis, which the author has studied long and carefully. A map and nearly one hundred and fifty illustrations add greatly to the value and attractiveness of the work.

MR. WINFRID A. STEARNS, a close student of natural history, and one of the authors of "New England Bird Life," has prepared a work entitled *Labrador: a sketch of its People, its Industries, and its Natural History*.[3] Although not written in a very agreeable style, the work is one which deserves perusal, and will certainly command some attention. Mr. Stearns visited Labrador three times, once in 1875, once in 1880, and again in 1882. The results of these journeys and observations are herein set down in a compact volume of three hundred pages. With the exception of a valuable paper on Labrador in the "Encyclopædia Britannica," little of a modern and useful character has been written giving anything like a fair description of the country and its resources. Mr. Stearns' book supplies the omission, and is cordially to be commended. It ought to pave the way for a good many excursion parties.

[3] Labrador: a Sketch of its People, Industries, and Natural History. By W. A. Stearns. Boston: Lee & Shepard. Price, $1.75.

MEMORANDA FOR THE MONTH.

THE reduction of letter postage from two cents per half-ounce to two cents per ounce, which took effect July 1st, suggests a few words in regard to postal matters in general. The collection of news by post-carriers is said to have originated in the regular couriers established by Cyrus in his Persian kingdom about 550 B. C. Charlemagne employed couriers for similar purposes in his time. The first post-houses in Europe were instituted by Louis XI. of France. Post-chaises were invented in the same country. In England in the reign of Edward IV., 1784, riders on posthorses went stages of the distance of twenty miles from each other in order to convey to the king the earliest intelligence of war. Post communication between London and most towns of England, Scot-

land, and Ireland existed in 1935. The penny-post was first set up in London and its suburbs in 1681 as a private enterprise, and nine years later became a branch of the general post. Mail coaches, for the conveyance of letters, began to run between London and Bristol in 1784. The postal system of the American colonies was organized in 1710. Franklin, as deputy postmaster-general for the colonies, established mail-coaches between Philadelphia and Boston in 1760. Previous to 1855 the rates of postage were according to distance. The uniform three-cent rate was adopted in 1863. Money-order offices were instituted in England as early as 1792. They were established in this country in 1864, and there is no safer way to remit small amounts.

THE
New England Business Directory
AND GAZETTEER
For 1885.

☞ *A very Valuable Book of Reference to every Business Man.* ☜

CONTAINING CAREFULLY COLLECTED LISTS OF THE

Merchants, Manufacturers, Professional and other Business Men throughout the six New England States, classified by Business, Town, and Post-Office.

ALSO

Banks, Savings Banks, Insurance, Manufacturing, Gas-Light and other Incorporated Companies, Post-Offices, Newspapers, Colleges, Academies, Expresses, Railroads, Together with other useful information often required in the COUNTING-ROOM.

A COMPLETE NEW ENGLAND GAZETTEER

Is a prominent feature of this edition, comprising a concise description of the Cities, Towns, Villages, and Post-Offices, showing Population, Telegraph and Railroad Stations, Money Order Offices, etc.

A Colored Map of New England Accompanies Each Book.

The whole forming a large Octavo Volume of 1892 pages, handsomely printed on fine paper, and substantially bound.

PRICE SIX DOLLARS.

Sampson, Murdock, & Co.,
(Formerly Sampson, Davenport, & Co.)

PUBLISHERS, 155 FRANKLIN STREET, BOSTON.

COOLIDGE HOUSE

BOWDOIN SQUARE, BOSTON.

The Coolidge is a centrally-located, thoroughly quiet and comfortable Family Hotel, with rooms arranged in suites, consisting of Parlor, Bedroom, and Bath; having an elevator, and combining all the luxuries and conveniences of the larger hotels, with the quietness and retirement of a private house; affording *most excellent accommodations at moderate charges.*

Coolidge Cafe,

Exclusively for Gentlemen.

Fitted up with the most complete and approved system of Broilers now in use, after the style of Spiers & Pond's Celebrated London Chop-Houses, and those so desiring, can select a steak or chop and see the same cooked on "The Silver Grill."

A Perfect Restaurant in Every Respect.

The Best Material, Cooking, and Service.

I. N. ANDREWS & CO.

STONINGTON LINE
INSIDE ROUTE TO

◁NEW YORK.▷

CONNECTING WITH

Philadelphia, Baltimore & Washington,

AND ALL POINTS

SOUTH AND WEST,
AVOIDING POINT JUDITH.

Via Providence and Stonington, connecting with the elegant Steamers

Stonington and Narraganset.

Express trains leave Boston & Providence Railway Station, Columbus Avenue and Park Square,

DAILY AT 6.30 P.M. (Sundays Excepted.)

Connect at Stonington with the above named Steamers in time for an early supper, and arrive in New York the following morning in time for the early trains South and West. *Ahead of All Other Lines.*

Tickets, Staterooms, etc., secured at

211 Washington Street, corner of State,

AND AT

Boston and Providence Railroad Station.

Regular landing in New York, Pier 31, North River. Steamer leaves the Pier at 4.30 P. M., arriving in Boston the following morning in ample time to connect with all the early Northern and Eastern trains.

A. A. FOLSOM, Superintendent B. & P. R. R.
F. W. POPPLE, General Passenger Agent.
J. W. RICHARDSON, Agent, Boston.

CARRINGTON'S BATTLES OF THE AMERICAN REVOLUTION.

WITH 40 MAPS.

BY COL. HENRY B. CARRINGTON, U.S.A., A.M., LL.D.

Cloth, $6. Sheep, $7.50. Half Calf (various styles) or Half Mor., $9 Half Russia or Full Mor., $12.

A. S. Barnes & Co., Publishers, New York and Chicago. Author's address, 32 Bremfield St., Boston, Mass.

THE FOLLOWING ARE EXTRACTS FROM MORE THAN 1,000 ENDORSEMENTS OF THIS VOLUME:—

To me at least, it will be an authority. A book of permanent value, not milk for babes but strong meat for men.—*Ex-Pres. T. D. Woolsey.*

Fills an important place in History, not before occupied.—*Wm. M. Evarts, N. Y.*

The maps themselves are a History, invaluable, and never before supplied.—*Henry Day, N. Y.*

An entirely new field of Historical labor. A splendid volume, the result of careful research, with the advantage of military experience.—*Geo. Bancroft.*

It is an absolute necessity in our literature. No one can understand the philosophy of the old War for Independence, until he has made a careful and thoughtful perusal of this work.—*Benson J. Lossing.*

The maps are just splendid.—*Adj. Gen. W. L. Stryker, N. J.*

The book is invaluable and should be in every library.—*Wm. L. Stone, N. Y.*

Of permanent standard authority.—*Gen. De Peister, N. Y.*

Indicates such profound erudition and ability in the discussion as leaves nothing to be desired.—*Sen. Oscar de La Fayette, Paris.*

I have read the volume with pleasure and profit.—*Z. Chandler.*

The volume is superb and will give the author enduring fame.—*B. Grats Brown, St. Louis.*

It should have a place in every gentleman's library, and is just the book which young men of Great Britain and America should know by heart.—*London Telegraph.*

The most impartial criticism on military affairs in this country which the century has produced.—*Army and Navy Journal.*

Fills in a definite form that which has hitherto been a somewhat vague period of military history.—*Col. Hamley, Pres. Queen's Staff College, England.*

A valuable addition to my library at Knowlsy.—*Lord Derby, late Brit. Sec. of State.*

A magnificent volume and a monument of national History.—*A. de Rochambeau, Paris.*

A godsend after reading Washington Irving's not very satisfactory Life of Washington.—*Sir Jos. Hooker, Pres. Royal Society, England.*

A book not only to be read, but to be studied.—*Harper's Magazine.*

The author at all times maintains an attitude of judicial impartiality.—*N. Y. Times.*

The record is accurate and impartial, and warrants the presumption that the literature of the subject has been exhausted.—*The Nation.*

Will stand hereafter in the front rank of our most valuable historical treasures.

The descriptions of battles are vivid. The actors seem to be alive, and the actions real.—*Rev. Dr. Crane, N. Y.*

We are all indebted to you for the labor and expense of preparing this volume, and I hope it will, in time, fully reimburse you.—*Gen. W. T. Sherman.*

Battle Maps and Charts of the American Revolution.

By HENRY B. CARRINGTON, M.A., LL.D., U.S.A.

Published by A. S. BARNES & CO., 111 & 113 William Street, New York.

The publishers issue this work for the use of teachers and scholars, as well as for its fitness as a companion to all Histories of the United States, with confidence that it will prove a valuable specialty to all.

The RED Lettering represents British Movements and Leading Topics, for the convenience of Teachers and Scholars.

The ¶ and Page references to various School Histories, which mention the Battles, make it available for use by Teachers throughout the United States.

The volume contains the 41 maps which were the result of thirty years of study, and are found in his standard volume, "Battles of the American Revolution."

The SECRETARY OF WAR has placed the "BATTLE MAPS AND CHARTS" at ARMY POST SCHOOLS, at government expense.

FIVE STEEL ENGRAVINGS of WASHINGTON accompany the volume. The ST. MEMIN (crayon) as frontispiece, engraved by Hall & Sons; also PEALE's painting (1772), HOUDON's bust (1784), TRUMBULL's painting (1792) and STUART's painting (1796) are furnished, in steel.

Price, $1.25. Sent, post-paid, to School Superintendents and Teachers, for introduction, upon receipt of $1.00. Liberal terms made with Schools, Military and Civil, Army Officers and Posts, State Militia, and the Trade.

NOTICES.

Invaluable to the student of American History.—*Baltimore (Md.) Herald.*

Deserves a welcome in every school district, as well as in every historical library in the land.—*Army and Navy Journal.*

In our opinion, General Carrington's work is an authority, showing great labor and careful study, and it should become a national text-book, and find a place in all public and private libraries.—*Indianapolis (Ind.) Herald.*

Each map is accompanied with a statement of the generals and number of men engaged on both sides, to which is appended the reason for such battle or engagement, with remarks by the author, who is excellent authority in military matters.—*The Educator (New Haven, Ct.).*

A valuable compilation from the author's large work, and cannot fail to make a more lasting impression upon the reader's mind than could be derived from the perusal of many volumes of history.—*N. Y. Herald.*

Each map is accompanied by a page of text, arranged upon a compact and original system, so as to present a singularly clear view of the history and significance of the engagement in question, the names of the chief and subordinate commanders, the forces, nominal and available, the losses on each side, and the incidents of the battle.—*N. Y. Evening Post.*

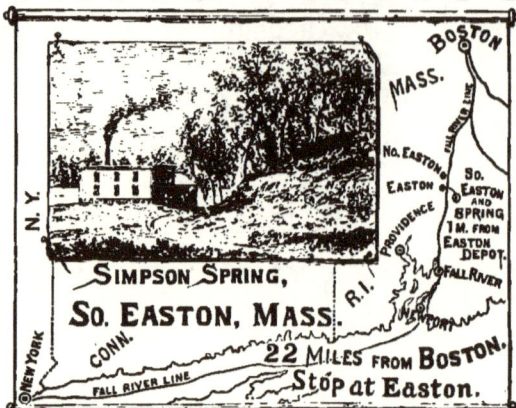

www.ingramcontent.com/pod-product-compliance
Lightning Source LLC
Chambersburg PA
CBHW021421090426
42742CB00009B/1201